THE HOME FRONT

PETER G. COOKSLEY

TEMPUS

This work is dedicated to the memory of four pioneers of modern historical military aviation research who, through their thorough approach and unceasing quest for accuracy, have raised the standards of aviation history immeasurably, and propelled it to a popularity it has never previously enjoyed:

J.M. Bruce, ISO, MA, FRAeS, FRHistS
Peter L. Gray
Bruce Robertson
Dr John W.R. Taylor, OBE, FRAeSs, FRHistS, AFAIAA.

They were also my friends.

First published 2006

Tempus Publishing Limited
The Mill, Brimscombe Port,
Stroud, Gloucestershire, GL5 2QG
www.tempus-publishing.com

British Library Cataloguing in Publication Data.
A catalogue record for this book is available from the British Library.

ISBN 0 7524 3688 0

Typesetting and origination by Tempus Publishing Limited
Printed in Great Britain

CONTENTS

By the Same Author:

ACKNOWLEDGEMENTS

The compilation of details for this book, a gigantic undertaking in itself, would have been even more daunting had it not been for the ready collaboration of a number of interested parties and experts, all with specialised knowledge. My sincere thanks, therefore, to these stalwarts and friends (any not thanked here are mentioned in the text):

Mrs Vera M. Brown who generously and immediately allowed me to photograph any item she had in which I expressed an interest.

Also Mike Cavanagh of Kettering Borough Council; Norman W. Cruwys, always resourceful and happy to share his knowledge; Roger Foukes who answered a single query with an impressive packet of valued material; Kenneth Harman for his encyclopaedic knowledge of obscure illustrations; T.C. Hudson, fellow writer, possessed of a wide knowledge of the demands of our craft; the late Harry M. Lyles who seemingly produced some rare artefacts from 'nowhere'; I. F. Mayhew who remembered for me his days as a gunner all those years ago; the late Bruce Robertson, generous to the end; Colin Withey who answered my appeals for help with good humour at a busy time, and supplied useful data on the rare searchlight trams; and not only the staff of the Imperial War Museum but also the staff of the Bexhill Museum of Costume, allowing me a rare 'rummage', which revealed something quite astonishing to both parties.

Finally, appearing at the end of this list only because it is compiled in alphabetical order, thanks to my helpful friends Richard Whittle and Harry N.R. Wylie.

Thank you all. I couldn't have done the job without you.

Peter G. Cooksley
London

INTRODUCTION

There have certainly been some excellent books in the past dealing with the men and machines pitted against each other in the struggle over England some ninety years ago, a struggle which was to condemn the civil population to a whole range of new and unique experiences. The general public not only had to come to terms with the constant threat of explosions, raging fires and being buried alive in their own homes, but also a host of domestic problems such as race riots, food rationing and coal shortages, which few books have covered. People also had to adapt to London's underground railway system, the increased work for police and fire brigades, and the growth of a large number of voluntary organisations, which inspired the founding of a 'marshall' system, forerunner of the air-raid wardens of the next war.

No less than seven exploratory attacks by airships had taken place between January and May 1915. The first sustained assault was carried out by LZ38 on the East End of London during the night of 31 May/1 June. The airship was initially accompanied by LZ27, but this second craft was later forced to return to base after being fired on by a 'mobile gun' in an aerial encounter. The airship LZ38, under Commander Linnarz, continued alone. Approaching from the north-west, carrying eighty-nine incendiary and thirty high-explosive bombs, the airship proceeded unopposed. The resultant death toll was seven, with thirty-five more civilians injured.

Of the following attacks in 1915, the most effective was on the night of 7 September, when ninety-seven bombs fell from LZ74 and SL2. An intended third raider, LZ79, was only able to contribute a single incendiary bomb, which landed on Fenchurch Street, having earlier wasted all but this last bomb on glasshouses at Cheshunt. Nevertheless, the two successful airships managed to start a large fire in the city, killing six men, six women and six children, and injuring thirty-eight. The following night saw 152 bombs dropped, wounding ninety-four and killing twenty-six (some reports state twenty-two), many of whom were passengers on two London buses.

Pomp and circumstance in June 1910, epitomised by King George V's Coronation procession as it passes under a Wellington Arch which is yet to receive its figure of Peace which we know today. (Author's collection)

Later, a more concerted campaign by conventional aircraft brought the total civilian casualties for the four year war to 670. It is a figure at which we, being of a more brutal generation, can scoff. After all, we can compare these civilian casualties with the much higher toll in the Second World War. However, to the people of the time, brought up to believe that an Englishman's home is his inviolate castle, the fact that innocent civilians were dying as a result of attacks on home soil was difficult to accept. The realisation triggered a massive moral shock as people saw that the dead were not just soldiers, fighting in a far-off land, but civilians, including women and children, in their own homes.

We now know that this was only a precursor to a future in which the scope of warfare was widened. Conflicts would never again be confined to encounters between trained fighting men in some far-flung clime, but would now involve large civil populations. These populations would not only have to live with the threat of death by shot and shell, but would also suddenly have to learn to cope with a new structure of existence, and the difficulties, privations, frustrations and dangers that this entailed.

Hanging over the besieged people of Britain was the spectre of shortages. The food shortage was the inspiration for this jingle, which describes a hopeful crowd queuing:

Outside a fast-closed door.
They think they'll get some sugar

For they've waited an hour or more.
But they're doomed to disappointment,
No sugar has arrived,
And their language, well 'twas shocking
When a card 'No Sugar' then advised!

This represents the good-natured acceptance of shortages and stress at work in the world of the wartime civilians. Yet a slow but constant increase in prices triggered widespread accusations of blatant profiteering, openly practised without attracting the attention of the law. Resentment grew, and stimulated reactions of a more serious nature, epitomised by the little-remembered protest march by the National Union of Railwaymen, one of the largest such demonstrations seen up to that date.

The extensive research in fresh directions that went into the compilation of this volume reveals how the new structure of existence gave a conflict between nations a dramatic new aspect as it was suddenly embraced those at home. This is the story of a people unexpectedly in the front line.

ONE

THE WAY IT WAS

To understand fully the background against which the first great war of the twentieth century was fought, it is necessary to go back to that period which marked the twilight of the civilians' peace. The dawn of the 1900s was greeted in much the same way as was the year 2000 in our own time; in an atmosphere of celebration and confident hope which, in 1900, drew its strength from the sense of security enjoyed by all island peoples, a feeling of safety and confidence inborn in generations receding into the mists of time, a product of the certainty that the Royal Navy was the country's 'sure and certain hope', and the belief that any wars were fought in trouble spots far away, by a superb and ever-victorious army.

Certainly the twentieth century was ushered on to the stage of time accompanied by reports of a troublesome but distant war in South Africa. However, both Mafeking and Ladysmith had been relieved by May 1900 and the nearest that the average Englishman came to encountering the reality behind the daily headlines was the return home of the CIVs – the City Imperial Volunteers towards the end of the year, after the successful taking of Pretoria.

In addition there were other strong but subtle contributions to the atmosphere of security, not least the fact that eighty-one-year-old Queen Victoria still occupied a throne which she had ascended in 1837. She had become a mother figure to most of the royal houses of Europe, so her death in January 1901 was seen by many as the end of an era. However, something of the spirit that had greeted the new century re-emerged to sweep 'Good Old Teddy' – Victoria and Albert's bluff, genial and democratic eldest son – to the throne as Edward VII.

In the wider world, where England's industrial might had built the foundation of the mightiest empire ever seen, technology and ingenuity were heralding such radical inventions as the cinema and the gramophone. Guglielmo Marconi had chosen to move his radio experiments from his native Italy to England, where he enjoyed the

Schutte-Lanz SL11, a wooden-framed airship which anticipated the use of 'Geodetic' construction some twenty years later. (Author's collection)

support of Sir William Pearce, the Postmaster General, with whom, on 12 December 1901, he established telegraphic contact with Newfoundland, 2,232 miles away.

Despite the fact that the Prince of Wales, King Edward's son, who was to succeed his father as King George V in 1910, had delivered a speech exhorting 'Wake up England!', there was soon no question that a fresh atmosphere was abroad which was spreading to many walks of life, including the young, who were flocking to take part in the new pastime of roller skating, where the indoor rinks were often illuminated by ever-changing coloured lamps, producing an effect not dissimilar to the strobe lights of today. For the older generation, one eagerly anticipated stage performance was the appearance of Lillie Langtry and her company, who were preparing her new play, written in collaboration with Hartley Manners, entitled 'The Crossways'.

Meanwhile, a newspaper had reported the Wright brothers' first flight, ending with the words: 'The idea of the box-kite was used in the construction of the airship'. However, the concept of aerial navigation was still rooted in the age-old idea of lighter-than-air vessels, and we see trials conducted at much the same time in Europe by a young man born on 8 July 1838 at Constance on the German-Swiss border. He was christened Ferdinand Adolf Heinrich, the son of Count Frederick von Zeppelin, a name which would become quite unjustly associated with military terror tactics. According to custom, Ferdinand joined the army, serving in the cavalry of the small kingdom of Wurttemberg in South Germany, distinguishing himself in the Franco-Prussian War of 1870–71, before taking leave of absence to journey to America, then plunged into civil war where, serving as an observer with the Federal Forces stationed in the vicinity of the Potomac, he quickly became interested in the use of Thaddeus S.C. Lowe's observation balloons.

Returning home, he attained the rank of Lieutenant-General before feeling compelled to leave the Army following loss of royal favour after the publication of a memorandum claiming that the Prussian military authorities dominated the forces of Wurttemberg. Now as a civilian he at last had time to interest himself in balloon work before extending his ideas to airships.

The year was 1890. Until this time airships had been little more than elongated balloons equipped with a motor-driven propeller, a type later to become known as 'non-rigids', and Ferdinand was to shed fresh light on the subject following suggestions that, in future, airships should consist of a series of individual hydrogen-filled compartments, in effect balloons, encased in a light metal framework covered in fabric, with propulsion supplied by a light petrol engine such as that recently perfected by Gottlieb Daimler.

The vessels which resulted soon became known as 'rigids', the world's first example being the LZ1, which made its maiden voyage in July 1900, the same month as the second season of the new Olympics Games, which opened on 2 July. The count's pioneering vessel was equipped with a curious control system, known as a 'sliding balance', which consisted of a rail, running the length of the 420ft vessel, on which ran a weight for horizontally trimming the airship. This turned out to be inadequate. An attempt to improve the arrangement for the next flight in the following October proved insufficient, and a new vessel was constructed. Like the first, it used twin engines. The new Zeppelin airship made its debut in 1906, and was initially known as LZ3, later becoming Z1 when accepted for the Army after re-building a year later. LZ24 was to become the first naval airship, with the identification L3.[*] In January two years later, von Zeppelin announced that he had commenced the construction of a commercial airship capable of taking 100 passengers.

As for the uses of the military vessel, it was to be employed primarily in the maintenance of continuous patrols, largely forgotten work which was soon to be overshadowed by their use as bombers in a war which was only three months away when L3 made her maiden voyage on 11 May. The acceptance of military airships after a development programme that seemed dogged by mishap, loss and tragedy, represented a personal triumph for Ferdinand, who had long advocated the use of rigid airships for the country's defence and security. It is strange, therefore, that the count was able to admit that a point was approaching beyond which airships were incapable of further development. With foresight, and a considerable amount of dignity, he could say that 'Airships are an antiquated weapon. Aeroplanes will control the air'.

However, although the name 'Zeppelin' from that time forward was to become erroneously applied as a generic term for all rigid airships, there were others,

---

[*] All Zeppelin airships were given a factory number prefixed by the letters 'LZ', those operated by the Navy being identified by the 'L' before their number. Army vessels adopted 'Z' before Roman figures. After 1915, normal (arabic) figures were used, the 'Z' being replaced by 'LZ'.

Rahere, jester and minstrel to Henry I is said to have founded St Bartholomew's Hospital in 1123, and is buried in the adjacent church. His tomb was one of the first to receive sandbag protection early in the First World War. (Author's collection)

including those from Luftschiffbau Schutte-Lanz, which were constructed from wood rather than metal, this according to the view of Professor Schutte-Lanz being more flexible than metal, and also lighter. It was an airship of this type, the SL11, that was the first airship to be brought down over England on 2/3 September 1916.

Ferdinand was to die in 1917. That same year the LZ104 appeared, a vessel which, in an attempt to fly relief to General von Lettow-Vorbeck, for three years besieged by Allied forces in German East Africa, was to finally complete a feat that would, in peacetime, have been described as record-breaking, having embarked on the long journey from Jamboli in Bulgaria on two previous occasions.

Back in Britain, the nation was undergoing a period of social upheaval. October 1903 saw the founding of the Suffragette movement. Baden-Powell held his first Scout camp on Brownsea Island, and this was quickly followed by the creation of the Girl Guides in 1907. However, there were other, more sinister, signs of social upheaval abroad; items began to appear in national newspapers about continued rioting in Tsarist Russia, indicating the emergence of a militant political fanaticism comparable in its nature to the religious fervour and political hatred stirred up in the Middle Ages. In England, the Suffragettes, part of a no less revolutionary movement, presented the more civilised face of change; from the back of a horse-bus in Trafalgar Square, they were selling pamphlets entitled 'Votes For Women', at one penny each.

ZEPPELIN BROUGHT DOWN IN FLAMES
AT CUFFLEY, NEAR ENFIELD, AT 2.30 A.M., SUNDAY SEPT 3rd 1916.
(DRAWN BY AN EYE-WITNESS)

The destruction of airship SL11 by Lieutenant W.L. Robinson on 3 September 1916 stimulated a flood of celebratory postcards such as this. (Author's collection)

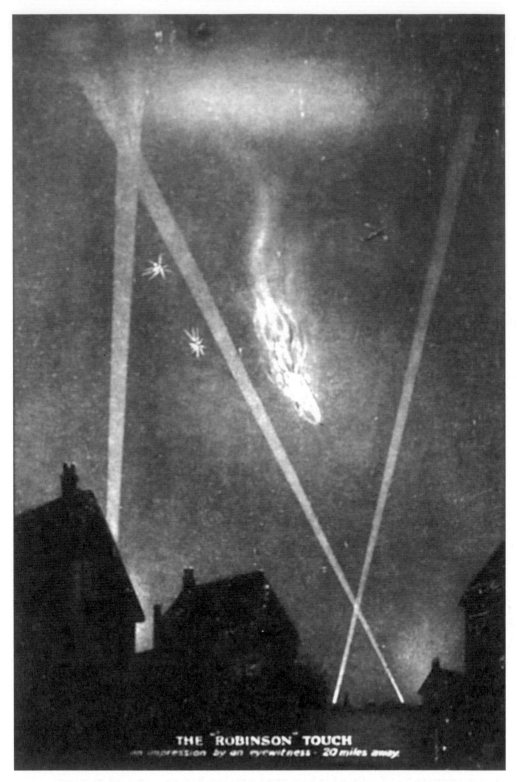

THE "ROBINSON" TOUCH
an impression by an eyewitness · 20 miles away.

Another artist's impression of the incident, said to be based on an eyewitness account from 20 miles away. (Author's collection)

Even photographs of Leefe Robinson's gun were circulated, this being the Vickers mounted ahead of the front cockpit, the rear one being covered over. Occupant is an RFC Air Mechanic. (via G.S. Leslie)

Lieut. William Leefe Robinson. V.C.

The announcement that Robinson had been awarded the Victoria Cross stimulated even more postcard mementoes, this one sent by Mr Sherwood to his son only a fortnight after the historic action. (Author's collection)

THE GREAT AIR RAID ON ENGLAND,
SEPTEMBER 3rd, 1916.

SOUVENIR PHOTOGRAPHS
OF THE WRECKED ZEPPELIN.

ALSO PHOTOGRAPH OF
LIEUT. WILLIAM LEEFE ROBINSON, V.C.,
WORCESTER REGIMENT & R.F.C.,
Who attacked the Zeppelin under circumstances of great difficulty
and danger, and sent it crashing to the ground as a flaming wreck.

COPYRIGHT.

In addition to cards, small souvenir booklets such as this appeared. (Author's collection)

Science, too, was blossoming in fresh directions as the twentieth century approached the end of its first decade. France had organised the world's first motor car race and, eight years later, in the United States, Henry Ford was to begin production of his Model 'T'. Submarines were now no longer a novelty; three years after the launch of Britain's first in 1901, six more were undergoing trials off Portsmouth in March, while in November one successfully crossed the Solent without surfacing. Of greater appeal to the civilian scanning his morning newspaper, however, were the announcements that science had discovered that the spread of yellow fever was due to mosquitos, and that acetyl salicylic acid, commercially known as 'aspirin', would be available for purchase 'over the counter' for the first time.

The opening years of the twentieth century were also to see the departure of many who had been household names, perhaps the best-loved being Florence Nightingale, in August 1910, who had revolutionised nursing in the Crimean War fifty-six years earlier. The new century had also claimed the lives of John Ruskin, the art-critic and social reformer, and that of Sir Arthur Sullivan, the musical genius who had contributed so much to the wit of W.S. Gilbert, with whom he had created the Savoy Operas. Gilbert was destined to outlive his colleague by eleven years, only to perish attempting to rescue a girl from drowning. The period also saw the passing of Henry Irving, the actor who had first impressed audiences in 1856. Meanwhile, an indication of the changes that were taking place in the theatre was the Berlin ban imposed on appearances by Iradora Duncan in the year following Irving's death: the American lady's lightly clad performances were deemed 'obscene'.

On the world's broader stage, it was now slowly becoming clear that while Britain and Germany were slipping into an accelerating arms race, the home of aviation development was regarded as France, a fact proven by Louis Bleriot's crossing of the English Channel in 1909 – an event that was greeted with a mixture of admiration and horror, for it was clear that the brief flight had, in some thirty-six minutes, destroyed for ever the centuries-old island atmosphere of invunerability, an attitude expressed by the newspaper columnist who was to mark the event with the prophetic, if premature, remark that perhaps 1,000 hostile aeroplanes could make a similar trip in five years time.

While the numbers suggested were completely wild, the implied date was something of an inspired guess. Another writer, wiser than most, dealt with the implications of the event in a column which he chose to head with the words 'England – an Island No More', and many would recall the Frenchman's crossing in the years to come, linking it in their minds with the appearance in Britain's skies during the following year of Halley's Comet, the ancient harbinger of disaster. Its sighting had troubled Britons over 800 years before, when the fiery omen had seemed to herald the fall of the old ways, after the defeat of the Saxons by the Norman army at Hastings in 1066.

Silk-embroidered cards were popular mementoes sent home by service men in France. Originally produced by nuns, the demand meant that the industry which provided them had to be expanded to include rural outworkers. (Author's collection)

Indeed it is interesting to speculate on just how far major events in the following years may have contributed to an almost superstitious pessimism about the future, with a succession of tragedies seeming like dark omens portending an even greater disaster. There was the death of C.S. Rolls, the aviation pioneer, in a flying accident at Bournemouth in the same year that he combined his name with that of Royce and began the manufacture of luxury cars. This was followed by the death of Captain Scott and his companions in the wastes of Antarctica while returning from the South Pole in 1912. Three months later – on 14 April – the world witnessed the loss of the White Star liner *Titanic*. But some expected an even greater catastrophe, on a worldwide scale, so much so that both the St John's Ambulance Brigade and the Red Cross were beginning to quietly prepare for an international war. Many predicted the likely source of such a conflict, with one commentator warning that 'a rupture between Germany and Britain would be an international calamity of the most disastrous kind'.

The final year of peace, 1913, was to be seen in retrospect as marking the end of an era. It was an era ushered in by American ragtime, and ruled over since 1910 by the new King George V, a hard-working but unimaginative man of simple tastes. It was neither Victorian nor Edwardian, it was unique, being remembered at home in connection with the adoption of domestic vacuum cleaners, Diaghilev's introduction of the Russian Ballet to London's theatre-goers, Chaliapin's magnificent tenor voice, the force-feeding of Suffragettes, and the introduction of 'revolutionary' fashions, which demanded that women wore dresses with trains for formal occasions, and wore hats crowned with piles of artificial fruit or lengthy ostrich feathers, while men should wear white tie and tails for dinner parties, black ties being reserved for formally dining at home. Europe hovered on the brink of war following events in the ever-troublesome Balkans, and the subsequent chain of events was to define the next era. However, many would remember the years up to 1913 fondly, albeit aware of those tragedies which darkened otherwise hopeful times.

It was in an attempt to prevent a souring of international relations that the Conference of Ambassadors was convened in London in 1913, with representatives of France, Germany, Russia and Austria present. The conference was chaired by Foreign Secretary Sir Edward Grey, a strange and largely ineffectual man who found the daily meetings an intolerable bore, being at heart a countryman who despised London life. His thoughts tended to drift constantly towards the pleasures of rural sports, particularly fishing, so that he took leave of absence in mid-April to devote a few days to them, leaving the chairmanship to the head of the Foreign office, Sir Arthur Nicolson. Despite amateurism such as this, on 30 May the Treaty of London was signed by Turkey and the Balkan states - only for there being a fresh outbreak of trouble in the area when two of the signatories went to war with each other in the following month.

Despite the little-publicised, perhaps little-known, distrust that some of the Conference delegates had for Grey, some being at least puzzled by him, believing that his air of 'marble calm' cloaked something more sinister, in Britain he enjoyed an active popularity, partly due, it is said, to his interest in all things rural. However, his attempts to be a politician may have had something to do with it, bearing in mind that the English are, supposedly, a people automatically supportive of the struggles of the amateur in a wide variety of fields…

These then were some of the events that were to shape the thinking and outlook of people who would mould the unimagined and unimaginable world of the opening years of the twentieth century, including the final cataclysm of the late summer of 1914 for which Sir Edward Grey, the British Foreign Secretary, must bear at least part of the blame, for he was a man who, despite being described later, by those who championed his policy, as doing 'everything to preserve peace', must be judged by history today, as being guilty of being amateurish, hesitant and inflexible, although this must be viewed in light of the fact that the British people and the Liberal Party were not united on the question of war. Henceforth, newspapers from the cheaper local echelons of the press would have to abandon what has been harshly described as content composed of 'melodramatic short stories of lurid crime and the supernatural', in order to feed an appetite for misery, fear and death that only the First World War would dull with reality' as a later writer described the situation.

The vast numbers of men required to wage war on a scale never before anticipated created a demand for high medical standards to be applied on a similarly huge scale. Just how variable these standards would be, however, was not at the time realised; standards were often lowered through slack application when shortages of manpower were most acute, so that even men with vision restricted by the loss of an eye were accepted, not only as Air Mechanics in the RFC, but even retained for flying duties, a case in point being that of Captain W.G.R. Hinchliffe, the RNAS pilot who continued to fly after a wound in combat impaired the sight of one eye. Standards were similarly slack when it came to discovering if a man suffered from colour-blindness, one candidate later recalling that the preliminary interview, which seemed to centre around his motivation rather than his medical condition, gave the young man plenty of time to devise a scheme whereby the discovery of his colour-blindness could be avoided. There are cases of men being accepted for the infantry in 1917 who had been rejected on three earlier occasions due to deficient sight.

Standards in other medical fields were often equally strange, a British fetish being the emphasis placed on a candidate's skill as a horseman, although this is not quite so ridiculous as it first appears: the 'good hands' required to guide a spirited horse have much in common with the sensitivity needed to control an aircraft.

Similarly there was the case of a young man, rejected by the medical boards of both the Army and the Navy, who was surprised by the friendly medical officer who attempted to cheer up the candidate by advising that the troublesome chest condition that had been the reason for his dual rejections would present no problem in the Royal Flying Corps, assuring him that the dry, cold air at a goodly altitude would benefit a recovery. It was only after he had been accepted for flying duties and had suffered a series of 'blackouts' while at the controls of an FE8 that he was transferred from active flying to the role of flying instructor!

However it must be admitted that, the authorities being aware of such anomalies, steps were taken to establish a common minimum medical standard for acceptance by the flying service, the central tenet of which was to discover those strong enough, or so the official report ran, to control an aircraft above an altitude of 20,000ft. In fact, modern standards dictate that everyone requires oxygen above 12,000ft!

Another aspect of the medical standards applied to pilots during the First World War was the policy by which men who had been severely wounded, perhaps in other branches of the Services, were not necessarily discharged, nor on recovery returned to their original branch. Instead, more than one man, deemed unfit for further duty, was surprised to find himself, often while still convalescing, transferred to the RFC, albeit for non-operational duties. Perhaps their role was often just to act as human ballast in the rear cockpit of a two-seater under test, but a certainty was that they would be a member of a unit in which medical care was represented by no more than a single Royal Medical Corps corporal, one of whom was attached to every squadron. The wounded from the trenches were a rich source from which these NCOs were recruited.

Gradually, despite the well-meaning efforts of the newspapers – the only effective 'media' of the day – to give a veneer of adventure, righteousness, glory even, to the obscene business of mass-killing, it became impossible to deceive the public further, and there resulted a massive wave of public desire to mitigate the horrors of war, which saw the founding of a vast number of organisations, great and small, by means of which ordinary people could feel that they were making a contribution to this desire, a yearning which soon spread beyond the bounds of nationality. Some of these strike one as bizarre today, such as the organisation calling itself The National Egg Collection for the Wounded, a society founded in 1916, with its headquarters at 154 Fleet Street EC4, and with Queen Alexandra, the widow of Edward VII, Victoria's eldest son, as its patron. This intended to rush newly laid eggs to wounded soldiers and sailors in base hospitals or collect funds to do so, it being described as 'pathetic to think so many eggs are going on to the market for ordinary consumption'.

Also possessing a comfortable, homely ring was the production of 'bazaar quilts'. These, sometimes known as 'sixpenny quilts', were often associated with church-based charitable organisations or Borough Needlework Associations and were often produced in patriotic red, white and blue. On payment of sixpence (3p), subscribers would be invited to autograph a piece of sheeting, the large signatures then being embroidered over and assembled after the fashion of a patchwork quilt. The finished article was then auctioned for War Savings.

The wounded were, of course, high on the list of deserving causes. Among the associations devoted to their comfort was the Hospital Supply Depots Service, its members meeting in each others' homes to make bandages and surgical dressings. Also notable were the War Hospital Supply Depots, with headquarters in Kensington. They carried out similar work, but extended the range of comforts to dressing-gowns and slippers.

Although many of these schemes were more popular with women, and therefore had a mainly female membership, the men who remained in Britain strove to support the soldiers too. The War Hospital Woodwork Depots allowed skilled carpenters to use their spare time to produce equipment such as bedside tables, book-rests, writing desks, cupboards, trays and, of course, crutches, all made from re-claimed wood that had been collected by the Boy Scouts. Other schemes designed to attract masculine skills included local Football Association Wounded Soldiers Funds which, from 1915, regularly sent boxes similar to those of the Red Cross Prisoners of War Fund to base hospitals, while the War Relief Committee used public donations to help fund hospitals. The Committee also helped to regulate the distribution of comforts provided by other organisations in a fair manner, as well playing a part in alleviating as far as possible local war-related distress.

The question of how best to help wounded servicemen produced many different answers; one organisation adopted the viewpoint that the boredom resultant from hospitalisation was a central problem and should be alleviated, and this resulted in the founding of the Military Hospital Wounded Soldiers' Entertainment Fund and the Hospital Men's Recreation Fund.

Other groups preferred to support the men of their own local regiments, so regimental Comforts Funds were created. An example is the Coldstream Guards Prisoners' Fund, established in August 1917 and administered by Mrs Christine Miller from its offices at 21 St James' Place, London, SW, while charity cricket and football matches, in which, for example, the police played the Army, were another source of revenue for good works.

There also existed charities to support a particular branch of the services, such as the British and Foreign Sailors Society, while others aligned themselves with either a political party or a branch of the Church. Prisoners of war were prominent among the beneficiaries of these, and two examples were the Women's Liberal Prisoners of War Fund and the Catholic Women's League. District affinities figured strongly, so that most areas held flag days to benefit local regiments via the County War Fund, an organisation with similar national aims as its equally large contemporary, the Prince of Wales National Relief Fund.

Additionally there were those which sought to do good on a wider basis, outside national parameters, one such being the London-based Russian Prisoners of War Help Committee, which aimed primarily to support those who had been captured by the Germans. However, this charity suddenly announced that, 'due to the revolution', it would disband, with effect from 15 January 1918. Two weeks before, the office at 18 Gloucester Place, Portman Square W1 finally closed its doors, after several years of useful assistance to Russian prisoners of war.

Among the oldest of the civilian wartime organisations was The Women's Service League, which was founded in August 1914, the same month as the declaration of war. This expected its members to 'solemnly pledge' to 'persuade every man I know to offer his services to his country' and to 'never to be seen in public with a man who, being in every way fit and free for service, has refused to respond to his country's call'. One wonders how men of fit appearance could visibly 'prove' that they had been rejected and how much bitter misgiving the members of this League later suffered when learning that their particular 'man' was dead or mutilated as a result of their subscribing to this particular form of social blackmail.

Less problematic was the League of Honour, an organisation 'For Women and Girls of the Empire' which expected its members to do 'all in their power to uphold and honour the Empire and its defenders by Prayer, Purity and Temperance', also promising 'to abstain from Alcoholic Drinks as beverage during the war, and to encourage others to do the same'.

Care for the requirements of women and girls also existed in the form of the Women's (later War) Emergency Corps. This too was of early foundation, having been created by a Miss Ransoke in October 1914. The services which it offered were many, but most important was the maintenance of a bureau to assist in finding employment for those ladies who had lost their jobs as a result of the war. At the same time the corps employed some women in its own workrooms, making toys which were eventually sold to finance its other activities, although this field was short-lived as women could increasingly find jobs created by men joining the forces. The WEC also ran service canteens and entertainment centres for soldiers and sailors, cared for refugees, and took charge of the personal belongings and valuables of men who had been hospitalised, since pilfering from wounded men was an ongoing, but little-publicised, problem. Valuables of wounded men who died were returned to the next of kin via the War Office.

There existed too flag-days entitled 'Blinded for You' and 'Crutch Day', both inaugurated in 1917, to raise funds in support of men who had suffered particular disabilities in battle. Also founded was the largely-forgotten Hospital Newspaper Fund. In addition, the sufferings of animals were remembered, the RSPCA War Fund holding street collections between 1915 and 1918 for veterinary care of horses, mules, dogs and other animals in war. In return for a coin in the collecting tin, contributors received a 'flag' showing a horse's head framed by an inverted horse shoe lettered with the title of the Fund. The Women's Emergency Corps also had a branch that provided for 'Wounded and Sick Army Horses'. There were huge numbers of horses killed in the war: 4,000,000 had perished by the end of the conflict. Most died as a result of sheer, bogged-down exhaustion, though of course horses also presented a bulky target for shell splinters, pistol, machine-gun and rifle fire.

The Girls' Friendly Society held fêtes to finance the provision of canteens, hostels and huts for the benefit of serving men, and the Church of England Army Huts charity had similar aims. A charity providing many soldiers with a welcome comfort was the General Cigarette Fund, which advertised that 'Every shilling [5p] subscribed means 50 large Virginia cigarettes for a soldier'.

Amateur theatricals were a popular way to comfort and entertain the soldiers, perhaps because they allowed first-hand contact with the men the performers sought to please. Particularly successful were the shows presented at Christmas and New Year, which were performed by adults and children alike.

Children were indeed amazingly swift to answer the call of charity. One school of children under ten years of age decided to begin growing vegetables and keeping livestock, rabbits and poultry. Many children made cheese, grew fruit (some of it later preserved), onions, carrots, French beans, lettuce, beetroots and potatoes, and it was to encourage enterprise such as this by young and old alike that the Ministry of Agriculture issued a mass of leaflets to encourage the keeping of small livestock, pigs and the setting up of market gardens, however small, by amateurs.

From as early as November 1914, some schools for both boys and girls were knitting comforts for soldiers and sailors, their output including balaclava helmets, gloves, scarves and sea-boot stockings. It was probably a slightly older relative of these children who is imagined by the composer of this tongue-tormenting jingle of the time:

> *Sister Suzi's sewing shirts for soldiers (saucy soft, short shirts our sister Suzi sews).*
> *And the soldiers sent epistles saying they'd sooner sleep in thistles*
> *Than the saucy, soft, short shirts, our sister Suzi sews!*

Meanwhile the St John's Ambulance Brigade and the British Red Cross had been meeting the challenge of the new demands with customary efficiency, while the Women's Reserve Ambulance Corps, formed in 1915 with equal quietude, but no less thoroughly, had been fulfilling its purpose of providing a force of trained, efficient and disciplined drivers to serve war hospitals and associated emergencies.

A pitiable sign of the resource shortages of the times was the employment of convalescent service men to produce utility envelopes from used newspapers. Society experienced radical upheaval as the government geared the country towards 'total war', and the strain on resources meant that scarcely a field of human activity in Britain was free from being used, in some way, to further the war effort.

Due to the urgent demands of the war, government assumed control over the nation at levels earlier undreamed of, as illustrated in the extreme measures it took to remedy a serious national timber shortage. During Question Time in the House of Commons in May 1917, Sir Frederick Banbury asked the Secretary for War, Ian Macpherson: 'Is the Honorable Member aware that the military are cutting down trees on Kenley Common [Surrey], some of which are eighty years old?' Macpherson replied: 'The trees have to be sacrificed because of urgent national necessity since it is planned to use the Common as an Aerodrome for defence against hostile raids by the enemy'.

The authorities even went so far as to deceive the public, albeit excusably, in 1917. As the autumn began, the nation was urged to collect as many horse chestnuts as possible. There was an official silence over the reason for this scheme, and speculation grew that these 'conkers' would form the staple diet of pigs. The actual explanation, however, was more subtle. At the outbreak of war it was suddenly realised that imports of acetone, a timber extract used in

REGISTRATION FORM

The Head of the Household should fill this in and return it to Harrods Food Bureau by TUESDAY, JANUARY 15th

I HEREBY declare that I have been a regular customer of Harrods for

MEAT   MARGARINE   BUTTER

(Cross out any item to which the statement does not apply)

and I am desirous of continuing to obtain, through Harrods, 'rationed' supplies of

MEAT   MARGARINE   BUTTER

(Cross out the articles not required)

and further I undertake, subject to my being registered for supplies of such article (or articles) at Harrods that I will not register elsewhere for the supply of such article or articles.

*Name in full*_____

Write clearly, stating Mr., Mrs. or Miss

*Give regular number to be provided for*_____

*Address in full*_____

_____

If you are an account customer } _____
please give number of your account }

If you obtain your sugar through Harrods } _____
give Pink number on your Old card }

HARRODS Ld   Woodman Burbidge
Managing Director   **LONDON SW 1**

A store's announcement before its introduction of rationing of certain commodities for its customers. (Author's collection)

the manufacture of nitroglycerine for producing cordite, would quickly vanish. Following experiments in 1916 it was discovered that a British source of this vital basic product was the humble conker and, as a result, factories were set up at King's Lynn and Poole. The first cordite produced by the new method became available in 1918.

Others remember the war years for more minor things, among them being the fact that in Britain the conflict was to usher in new bank-notes to augment the already-established white 'flimsies' (five pound notes). There were only two new types of note, one intended to replace the gold sovereigns (one pound) long in circulation, and the other the half-sovereigns (ten shillings, or 50p to our generation). They were printed on the same quality paper as stamps, in a rather gaudy and distinctly unofficial-looking pattern, and quickly became known as 'Bradburys' due to the signature of John Bradbury, the Secretary to the Treasury at the time, being printed in the lower, right-hand corner. The first steps of this transition took place when banks re-opened after the 1914 August Bank Holiday, when gold coins began to be called in and replaced by paper notes. Inicdentally, the original designs were short-lived, being replaced on 26 August of the following year, their design deemed 'too easy to forge'.

This was also the age which saw Harrods of Knightsbridge anticipate later government policy by introducing meat, margarine and butter rationing for its customers. Two pounds of meat per head and four ounces of either margarine or butter were allowed. The scheme received its preliminary announcement in *The Times* during 1917, with details a year later, on 11 January 1918, specifying that such measures would begin ten days later, the last day for registration being 15 January.

All such measures combined to destroy for ever the Britain which had been indirectly 'shot dead', along with the remainder of Europe, by the pistol of Gavrilo Princip, member of the foolish but dangerous Black Hand organisation in Sarajevo. Certainly to those of us who never knew it, one gains the impression that for some, the era preceding the First World War offered a peace and contentment that was to be denied to later generations.

During this era the press was the only method of mass communication and, not needing to compete so desperately for sales as it does today, it did not need to resort to vehement political allegiance, exaggeration or the spreading of alarm and despondency in order to survive commercially. The result of this was that ignorance created bliss before the dawn of the age of turmoil. This too was a Britain where men answered the call to arms with a total sense of conviction which is, in some ways, incomprehensible to us now. These same young men, counted 'steady, gentle and responsible' in civilian life, often surprised and horrified their friends and families on returning home, by revealing the pride they took in killing, boasting that they could put up such rapid fire from the trenches that the enemy thought they had been issued with automatic weapons, and recounting stories of close combat in a trench-raiding club... a 16in hammer shaft with 3in of one-eighth lead wrapped round the head and nailed and secured by a few nails made a lethal killing mace...

Private Wilfred F. Browne of the Gloucesters, one of the men sent to protect the East Coast against an anticipated invasion. (Author's collection)

Attitudes such as these, unthinkable even months before, were absorbed by civilians from men returning from the Front. The sense of unease added to the domestic strain caused by the fear of invasion. Though the island people scarcely spoke of their fear, they were having to cope with its implications for the first time since the Napoleonic wars of some ninety years before. In those days, however, the lack of speed suffered by communication softened the potential blows brought by news. Now the atmosphere was all one of urgency, and with it came fear.

One source of alarm was the fear that the enemy would attempt a landing on British soil. Indeed, there was a protracted period during which a substantial body of soldiers was retained to defend the east coast, one of the areas where an attempted invasion might be expected, and it was only to make good the hideous losses on the Western Front that these men were ultimately dispersed and sent to replace their fallen comrades.

NATIONAL

REGISTRATION

ACT, 1915.

A civilian identity card issued following the introduction of National Registration in 1915. They were smaller than those of 1939–45 and buff in colour. (Author's collection)

But it was not only on the eastern seaboard that an invading force might be expected; many, including such distinguished tacticians as Lord Derby, the Secretary for War, and Lord French, believed that Dover, due to its geographical position, was a potential danger spot where a serious invasion attempt might be made, or if not, at least a final, desperate push.

The seriousness with which these possibilities were discussed is illustrated by the regulations drawn up by the Home Office, which describe the procedures to be followed in such an event. In some areas, Lincolnshire for example, these plans were given wide publicity, particularly to farmers, who would have to know in advance what to do with their livestock, vehicles and the like. The directives go into great detail, stating by which roads the movement of animals was to take place and which towns had been selected as reception centres.

Dover, on the other hand, despite its strategic position, followed a policy of silence, taking the view that publication of the Home Office plans would alarm its inhabitants unnecessarily, especially if they were made overly aware, for example, of such details as the instruction for Special Constables from outlying villages to be prepared to collect and drive all cattle into the centre of the town once the alarm had been confirmed and raised.

If it was decided to evacuate the whole or part of the town, huge groups consisting of probably many thousands of civilians were to be accompanied by mounted police officers and were to be directed to one of the ten reception centres, each catering for their own area of Dover, which had been divided into the same number of sectors. The plans even showed the routes by which refugees were to travel in order not to impede troops hastening to repel the invaders.

As history is aware, it was never necessary to adopt these draconian measures, although at the time of the enemy push towards the Channel Ports, in October 1914, notices were distributed to every household which headed 'The inhabitants of Dover are informed that under Military Orders they are to evacuate the town IMMEDIATELY' before going on to summarise provision 'as far as possible' of transport for those unable to walk, and adding that all should 'carry warm clothing and sufficient food and drink for twelve hours'.

In fact, at the same time that it was anticipated that these notices would have to be issued, Dover was already undergoing a different form of 'invasion'; beginning

In order to raise money for the Belgian refugees coming to Britain, the village of Gretton raised a jazz band in 1915. Suitably dressed, they posed for this photograph. (Courtesy Roger Fowkes)

in September, it was still in full-flow a month later. It consisted of thousands of Belgian refugees, in the main travelling via Ostend and Dieppe. They were at first diverted to Folkestone but, between 10 and 17 October, the main thrust began to move towards Dover. The refugees numbered an estimated 13,000, including 5,000 wounded Belgian soldiers. These vast numbers used almost any type of available vessel to cross the Channel, ranging from those with such familiar names as *Invicta* and *Queen*, 'packed to the limits of their capacity', to fishing smacks, their occupants being 'half-perished with cold and hunger', possessing 'nothing in the world but what they carried in their hands and wore on their backs' according to a contemporary writer. However, according to popular allegations at the time, these hordes of pitiable humanity included twenty spies, so that an exclusion order was issued with the intention of excluding all foreigners from the town. Whatever the truth of this tale, by 14 November all had vanished from Dover's centre except for two, who had allegedly been granted special permission to remain. This atmosphere of suspicion was probably responsible for the town being designated a 'special military area', which meant that entry by road or rail was allowed only if the traveller held a special pass. Around 22,000 of these passes had been issued by 11 October 1915, the date on which it was announced that the National Registration cards, introduced in the summer of that year, were henceforth regarded as sufficient identification.

TWO

AIRSHIPS AND COUNTER-MEASURES

In political circles, the outbreak of the First World War was not a particularly surprising turn of events. The Cabinet was still opposed to a European conflict, but some politicians had begun to take a broader view; as the summer of 1914 advanced, it became clear that there was little time remaining in which to prepare if the worst happened.

Among the members of the government who took this viewpoint was the forty-year-old Winston Spencer Churchill, First Lord of the Admiralty, who, as early as Monday 27 July, having first gained permission from Prime Minister Asquith, set about the provision of armed guards for the country's ammunition and oil stores, before looking into the question of collecting what the nation had in the way of defensive aircraft and basing them in the region of the Thames Estuary in anticipation of Zeppelin attacks.

The likelihood of something of this nature quickly developing once the war had officially started soon occupied other minds, as was made clear by a letter received by Churchill on 28 August. This came from H.A. Gwynne, editor of the *Morning Post*, who begged to present a scheme involving bomb-carrying balloons which would be released into the paths of Zeppelins, detonating on any collision. Incidentally, ideas of this nature were to come from various persons from time to time over the next four years!

There were other suggested methods of combating the airship menace, one of Churchill's being that the Royal Naval Air Service should establish a base at Dunkirk, supervised by Commander Samson, and be equipped with aeroplanes which could be swiftly scrambled to attack enemy airships en route to Great Britain. Provision for the defence of this base would be a fleet of armoured cars, which could also be used for establishing other bases up to a distance of 100 miles inland.

Meanwhile, as a result of a request from Kitchener that the Admiralty take full responsibility for the aerial defence of Great Britain with effect from 3 September,

Commander Samson RN, with a group of English flyers at Amiens in 1915. He led more than one daring attack on the bases of aircraft used to raid the British Isles. (Author's collection)

an inventory was demanded of all anti-aircraft guns deployed for the defence of the capital, land-based, on temporary or permanent sites, or on naval vessels.

In addition it was deemed necessary to create a force of interceptors, 'within range of a line drawn from Dover to London', based at Calshot, Eastchurch and Hendon, together with a number of Emergency Landing Grounds, which were to be lit at night, marked with prominent white circles during daylight, and have all obstructions, such as railings, removed.

The majority of these measures, which were surprisingly comprehensive in view of the fact that mankind's ability to fly was under eleven years' old, were not to be confined to the protection of London alone. Another potential target for an enemy air attack was the Grand Fleet, then lying at Loch Ewe in Scotland. However, it proved almost impossible to supply a force of aircraft to protect the fleet, and many an official sigh of relief was no doubt to be heard when the Fleet set sail.

Nevertheless, few lost sight of the fact that the best form of defence lay in attack, and four British aircraft based at Ostend were accordingly designated as a potential force for bombing enemy airship sheds at Dusseldorf and Cologne. On 22 September, the aircraft flew their first such sortie from Antwerp, the nearest base to German territory. A second attack took place on 9 October, with the result that one Zeppelin was destroyed in its shed. Sixteen days later there were unsubstantiated reports of a sighting of a Taube monoplane off Dover, and many anticipated an attack.

So, while such decisive measures as the attacks on the airship sheds were making history, the enemy was not to prove idle; a Friedrichshafen FF29 floatplane (No.203), the aircraft erroneously reported as 'a Taube', confirmed fears of an attack by announcing its arrival with 'two heavy reports' at 'about mid-day'. To be precise, the time was exactly at 1 p.m. on Monday 21 December when a couple of bombs fell into the sea west of Admiralty Pier. In the minds of the public, this was an outrage equalled only by the shelling of Hartlepool, Whitby and Scarborough by German battle-cruisers five days earlier, an assault which had followed an exploratory attack on Great Yarmouth on 3 November, although in general the attitude of the public at this stage was one of calm acceptance.

However, after that attack on the Monday of Christmas week, other raids were to materialise, all of which were to be reported in detail by the newspapers appearing on Boxing Day, under such headlines as: 'THREE GERMAN AIR RAIDS: Machines attacked by British Aviators over Sheerness & Southend' and 'ENEMY BOMBS ON DOVER: One Aeroplane Hit Three Times: All Chased to Sea and Escape'. There followed a report dealing with the visitation of another Friedrichshafen FF29 floatplane, this time No.204, from the same unit as the earlier one – See Flieger Abteilung 1 from Zeebrugge – which ran: 'Christmas Eve brought England her first experience of aerial invasion. A German airman appeared over Dover at about 11 a.m. [actual time has since been variously described as between 10.45 and 10.55 a.m.] on Thursday and dropped a bomb which exploded harmlessly in a garden about 400 yards from the Castle'. The weather was described as 'foggy and cloudy'.

The enemy aircraft had been seen approaching from the direction of Deal. The garden where its single bomb exploded was owned by a Mr Thomas A. Terson, JP, a local auctioneer and valuer, and it stood just behind St James' rectory. An eyewitness, Mr Mowell, from a family of well-known local solicitors, who was at the time talking to a friend in the street, not only heard the 'screech' of the falling bomb but, looking up, 'saw the last 200 yards of its fall'. Meanwhile, the cook working in the rectory kitchen was showered with broken glass, though otherwise unharmed, and a gardener outside, gathering greenery for Christmas decorations with the aid of a 20ft ladder, was to fall from it, alarmed by the sudden sound of the explosion.

The resultant crater left by the bomb was described as being 10ft across and 3 or 4ft deep, while windows were broken not only in the rectory, but also 200 yards away and in nearby Maison Dieu Road. A 'large fragment' of the 22lb missile was discovered on the veranda of a house in Victoria Park and, although a Wight floatplane and a Bristol TB8 from the East Promenade and Eastchurch respectively were both sent to attempt to intercept the raider, no sighting was made, and return to base was made at 11.45 p.m., after a twenty-five-minute search.

The same Bristol machine was aloft again on the following day in company with a Vickers FB4, this time with the intention of destroying Freidrichshafen FF29 203, which had appeared again on Christmas Day, 'very high' (7,000ft) at 12.35 p.m., over Sheerness. Reports claimed that the crews of the two British aircraft intercepted the raider and scored hits 'three or four times' before losing contact. The enemy was certainly also hit by Sheppey's anti-aircraft guns, before the crew, losing height a little, made their unhurried way up the Thames as far as Gravesend and, retracing their course, bombed Cliffe railway station an hour later, the earlier thick fog having now dispersed.

All this is known from a number of fragmentary reports, and it is difficult to reconcile these facts with a newspaper reference to 'Two enemy aircraft ... at about 6,000 feet' making 'great speed towards the north' which were met with 'a fusillade [from the ground which] began at 10c [1 p.m.] and lasted a quarter of an hour', from the vicinity of Southend. That the second machine was a British aircraft in pursuit is a valid interpretation, and it has certainly been alleged that the raiding aircraft returned to base with damaged fuselage and floats.

These initial attacks were all carried out by aeroplanes, and this seemed to contradict the widely held belief that the principal instrument of attacks on targets in Britain would be the much-vaunted airships. Such rumours had been sparked after the successful duration flight in Germany in 1908 of a Zeppelin. However, by the outbreak of war in August 1914, only five such vessels were available for military purposes in the west. A huge construction programme had been launched, with a target of sixty-one airships, but it was Z6, one of the earliest examples, that was pressed into service, bombing the Liege forts on 6 August. However, as if to highlight the vulnerability of the craft to gunfire, the Zeppelin was hit and crashed in a forest near Bonn.

At this time aerial bombs as such did not exist, and artillery shells were used instead. It was estimated that Z6 only had the ability to lift about four, although the

Incendiary bomb dropped on Charlton Road Fire Station in September 1915 which failed to ignite. (Peter Lamb collection)

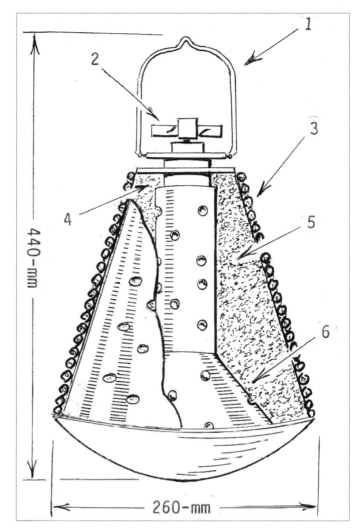

Sectional view of an incendiary bomb.
1. Carrying handle to which some had a 1m x 6cm streamer attached.
2. Ignition arming propeller with inertia fuse beneath.
3. Impregnated rope binding.
4. Perforated central brass column containing Thermite detonating mixture.
5. Resinous incendiary mixture of Thermite, Benzol and tar.
6. White phosphorous mixture in lower part of central column.
(Photo and drawing, author)

situation was remedied by September when proper bombs had been developed, 2,000lb being dropped by night on Antwerp.

The first airship attack on Britain was also a night sortie, carried out six days after permission had been granted by the Kaiser on 19 January 1915. The raiding force consisted of L3 and L4; L6, which was supposed to have been included in the force, had to return to base with engine trouble, the remaining pair being seen by observers as 'two bright stars moving apparently thirty yards apart'. Great Yarmouth was to receive six high explosive bombs and seven incendiaries from L3, while King's Lynn received the bulk of the load of the lost L4. In all, six persons were killed and two unsuccessful defence sorties were mounted. A proposed attack six days earlier had been prevented due to the weather.

Of the nineteen airship attacks on Britain in 1915, the attack on 31 May 1915 was the most historically significant, as a change had been made in the Kaiser's earlier orders to his men. The change was the result of advice from less civilised counsels, so

Policy No. A 12390

Government Insurance against Aircraft Damage

issued by the

ESSEX & SUFFOLK EQUITABLE INSURANCE SOCIETY, LTD.,

ESTABLISHED 1802.

Head Office : The Fire Office, Colchester.   London Office : 56 to 62, New Broad Street, E.C.,

as Agent for His Majesty's Government.

Premium £ = :4 :=

   This Policy of Insurance made the *Twenty seventh* day *of November.* 19*15*
Witnesseth that in consideration of *W. E. Baker.*
(hereinafter called the Insured) paying to HIS MAJESTY'S GOVERNMENT (hereinafter called the
Government) the premium above mentioned, for insuring as hereinafter mentioned, the following property,
viz. :—

   (*a*)   On

and/or

   (*b*)   On the property or several items of property described, and
          each of the matters specified, in the Fire Policy
          No. *42721*   effected by the Insured with
          the ESSEX & SUFFOLK EQUITABLE INSURANCE SOCIETY, LIMITED, for £ *2 00 : = : =*
          the sum or several sums thereby insured thereon.

   The Government agree with the Insured (subject to the terms and conditions expressed hereon, which are
to be taken as part of this Policy) that if after payment of the premium the above-mentioned property or any
part thereof, shall be destroyed or damaged directly or indirectly by AERIAL CRAFT (hostile or otherwise)
or Shots, Shells, Bombs or Missiles from or used against Aerial Craft at any time before four o'clock in the
afternoon of the day of *27th November.* 19*16* the Government will pay or make good all such
loss or damage within 30 days after it has been adjusted to an amount not exceeding in respect of the
several matters the subject of this Insurance the sums hereby insured thereon respectively and not exceeding
in the whole the sum of *Two hundred.* pounds.

   In Witness whereof I, being an Official of the ESSEX & SUFFOLK EQUITABLE INSURANCE SOCIETY,
LIMITED, have hereunto set my hand.

For His Majesty's Government.

Against a premium of 4s this householder insured his property against aircraft damage to the value of
£200 in November 1915. (N.W. Cruwys' collection)

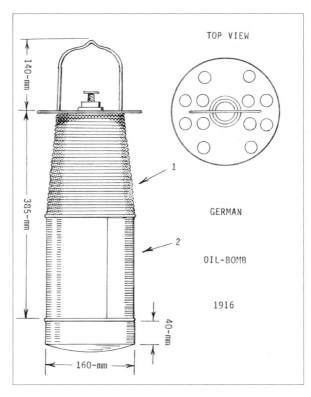

Enemy oil bomb complete with carrying handle.
1. Rope-bound incendiary section.
2. Oil container.

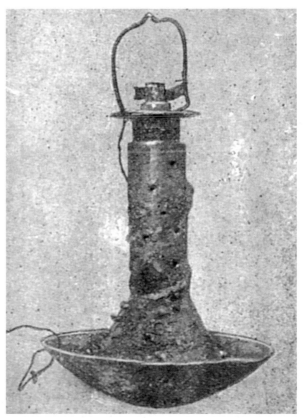

Burnt-out incendiary bomb.
Zeppelins carried about fifty of these.
(Author's collection)

that among the stipulations withdrawn were those forbidding attacks which might damage royal palaces, historical buildings and private homes. The attack carried out at the end of May was the first mounted against London under these revised orders, and the raid targeted previously banned sites east of the Tower.

Although only two airships were involved in this, LZ37 and LZ38 flying from Belgium, the measured beat of their motors, typical of their kind, would soon become familiar to Londoners, and were not dissimilar to those associated with the enemy raiders of twenty-five years later.

Today, this attack is chiefly remembered by the historians of London for two reasons. Firstly, the raid ultimately resulted in an attempt to completely silence Press reports of the attack beyond the publication of official communiqués. Secondly, to a later generation it was of interest to learn that among the interceptors, flying as a gunner on this occasion despite being a qualified pilot, was Royal Naval Air Service Flight Sub-Lieutenant Ben Travers, a figure later to win theatrical renown as the author of the Whitehall farces of the 1940s.

It rapidly became clear over the following months that attacks by enemy airships indicated a new dimension in warfare, but this was not accepted with equanimity. Lord Balfour, Foreign Secretary to the wartime coalition government, later claimed that London was an undefended city with poor defences, only to be countered by Zeppelin commander Heinrich Mathy: 'If Balfour had stood by my side and looked at those flashing guns everywhere, he would not have said that London was a militarily undefended city and perhaps not think so poorly of its aerial defence'. Nevertheless, it was true that, in those early days, London's defences were abysmally feeble, and those people who could afford to do so seized their every chance to leave built-up areas which lay in range of enemy airships.

This fact was quickly seized upon by providers of rural and coastal holiday accommodation. A typical advertisement appearing in a newspaper of 1915 ran:

DON'T WORRY ABOUT THE RAIDS but go to CLIFTONVILLE for your Easter Vacation, one of the safest and best protected resorts on the coast. The air is unrivalled, and there is every attraction for visitors. Excellent accommodation can be obtained at CLEVELANDS, 310 Northdowns Road, Cliftonville, Margate. Easter Terms – Thursday evening until Tuesday morning, 25/- inclusive. Tariff on application.

Meanwhile, part of London's population was learning to cope with bombing attacks, a theatre 'prospectus' of the same period declaring:

NOTICE. Arrangements have been made that warning of a threatened air raid will be communicated by the Military Authorities to this theatre… On receipt of such a warning the audience will be informed, with a view to enable persons who may wish to proceed home, to do so… The warning will be communicated, so far as possible, at least twenty minutes before any actual attack can take place. There will, therefore, be no cause for alarm or haste… Those who decide to leave are warned not to loiter about the streets, and if bombardment or gunfire commences before they reach home, they should take cover.

The theatre warning was timely, as on the night of 13 October 1915 the airship L15, part of the most ambitious attack on the capital so far, dropped bombs which damaged the Lyceum Theatre in Wellington Street and the Strand Theatre in Catherine Street, killing twenty-one and injuring thirty-six persons. Some began to realise the pressures experienced in parts of the East End, where many felt neglected by out-of-touch authorities, with the result that police were vigilant for signs of rioting.

Some in the East End were confused as to where these new raiders had suddenly appeared from; some at the time failed to appreciate that the air was a connecting ocean between the Continent and the British Isles, and when a lady remarked to her cleaner how dreadful it was that foreign airships could invade England's skies, she received the reply: 'Don't you believe it, Ma'am, they come from the yard behind the grocers with a foreign name in the High Street!'

Crews of these lighter-than-air bombers, quickly and universally referred to in Britain as Zeppelins, ignoring the Schutte-Lanz vessels mostly operated by the Army, quickly became efficient at flying to their tactical advantage, climbing as soon as possible to an altitude where the prevailing easterly winds were beneficial in good weather on nights when there was little moon, and shutting down their engines over the target area in order not to attract the attention of searchlight operators. As operational experience began to influence design, improved vessels entered service, culminating in the 'Super-Zeppelins' – airships which were powered by seven Maybach motors and which could carry a bomb load of perhaps 8,000lb (3,630kg) at speeds in excess of 80mph (130km/h).

It was from an earlier example of the raiding Zeppelins that a specimen survives of an observation car. These were small gondolas, today often described as 'spy-cars' or 'baskets', which were trailed on several thousands of feet of wire from a Zeppelin safe above cloud, designed to allow the car-observer below the cloud cover to give directions over a telephone to the 'mother' vessel, identifying targets before the bombs were released. This one example is held in the care of the Imperial War Museum in London. The observation car was said to have been dropped together with some 5,000ft (1,524m) of cable from LZ90 on the night of 9 February 1916, when sixteen of the eighteen airships despatched appeared over East Anglia. That this evidence exists comes as something of a surprise, since it has been alleged in some quarters that these cars were only adopted when improved defences ultimately forced raiding dirigibles to operate at heights up to 25,000ft, where the crews lacked oxygen as well as suffering from intense cold. The preserved car was 'discovered by a farmer next morning together with hundreds of yards of connecting wire', according to contemporary reports. The specimen referred to, which was acquired by the museum in 1921, is an aerody-namically-shaped gondola and, despite gruesome reports that it was discovered containing the mutilated body of the unfortunate observer, was in fact empty, bearing signs of having 'run away' with the winch operators and been lost. On being discovered, it was first put on display with other air raid memorabilia at the Finsbury Headquarters of the Honourable Artillery Company at the end of

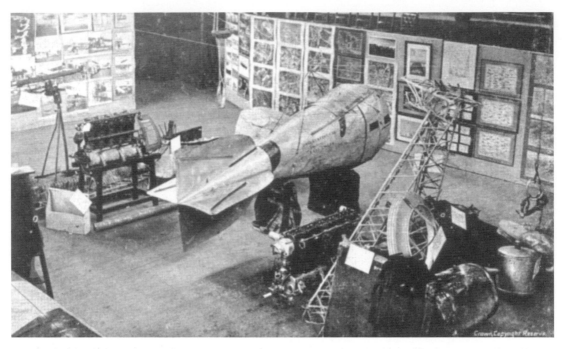

Observation car from Airship LZ90 discovered in a field 2/3 September 1916 at Manningtree, Essex. It is seen here probably on display at Crystal Palace having been previously on show at Finsbury and is now exhibited in the IWM. (Author's collection)

1916 where many of those who saw it would have been surprised that it bore no resemblance to the rectangular bullet-proof cages containing two men of popular illustration as early as the closing months of 1914.

The first attack by Zeppelins on British targets had taken place on 13 January 1915. Three airships were earmarked for this first assault, most likely being L3, L4 and L6. The squally conditions forecast for the first intended night meant that it was postponed until six days later. The three vessels set out, the first pair setting course for Norfolk, the last, intended for the Thames Estuary, having to return to base with engine trouble while still nearly 100 miles from the English coast. Of the remaining pair, L3 crossed at Ingham at 8.05 p.m. in conditions that had now become foggy with some rain. A number of parachute flares were dropped so that the airship's crew could assess their position.

It was only a little later that Mr W.J. Sayers of Great Yarmouth together with his son, both returning home from choir practice, were startled to see above them a bright light. They became aware that some sort of aircraft was overhead, and suddenly heard the sound of something falling towards them. Before they found time to fully react, a pair of bombs exploded behind the pair, flinging both to the ground, the shoulder of the younger man being pierced by a splinter. A further four 110lb bombs, plus a number of incendiaries, were to complete a night's work for L3, which then set course for Fuhlsbuttel at 10 p.m., landing back at base at 9.40 a.m. the next day, leaving two dead, one man and one woman, as a result of its visit.

The companion airship, L4, had crossed the coast five minutes before L3, at Mundesley. A little later the airship dropped a pair of bombs at Sheringham, before flying along the coast, its captain seemingly attracted by the lights of King's Lynn, on which were loosed seven high explosive bombs and six incendiaries, damaging a number of homes and killing a woman and young boy. The captain then set a course that took the Zeppelin over Great Yarmouth and then out to sea en route to its base, where it landed at 9.45 a.m. the following morning.

Only two defending aircraft were sent up to intercept the raiders, a pair of Vickers Gunbus machines from 'C' Flight, No.7 Squadron at Joyce Green, Kent, when it was believed that London was the intended target. The crews had been ordered to patrol south of the capital, thus no sightings of the enemy were made, although it is doubtful if the airships would have been visible even if the two-seaters had been better deployed, the weather conditions seeming to favour the raiders entirely. This being so, it is surprising to note that no further enemy attacks were mounted for a period of some three months, until Tyneside and the Humber area were visited on consecutive nights and history was made in the notorious London raid mentioned earlier.

The following autumn, the night of 13/14 October was to be the most eventful of the year. Among the group of four Zeppelins sent against London on that night was L15, commanded by Kapitan-Leutnant Joachim Breithaupt, this being his third raid on England and his first on London. He remembered that sortie for

The 15ft-diameter Kilnsea sound mirror is believed to be of pre-1918 vintage and intended to cover the course followed by airships intending to attack Hull. (Courtesy Charles Parker)

the ease with which it was possible to pick out such landmarks as Regent's Park, the Serpentine, Tottenham's 'seas of houses' and Waterloo Bridge from 11,000ft. This was a worrying altitude, but it had to be accepted as the air was warmer than expected, making it impossible to climb further with bombs aboard. It was a relief, therefore, to drop some 'in a stick which caused damage in a long line stretching from Hyde Park down to Limehouse in the docks area'. The attack had been preceded by a period of waiting with engines idling, listening for the sounds of defending aircraft.

Two reports dealing with the attack of 15 October survive, the first of these being that made by the thirty-two-year-old Heinrich Mathy, an officer from an old Baden family and at the time in command of L13. He was an experienced officer who had joined the Navy in 1900, transferring to airships three years later. Briefly reverting to torpedo-boats, he finally settled with airships in 1915, where he was quickly to become hero-worshipped by comrades and public alike due to his skill as a cool tactician. Of the attack on London he was to write:

About 11 a.m. on 14-10-15, L10 received by telephone the order 'Attack London'; and the same order was also sent to L11, L14, L15 and L16. Takeoff ensued at 1.40 p.m.

In order to avoid collision, L13, as the senior commander's vessel gave the signal by wireless: 'Attack course to be E-NE, return course, NE. Report by wireless immediately after the attack'. These orders then concluded with the altitude to be flown and the name of the Commander, by way of a signature.

Ammunition taken aboard was 1 x 300kg and 20 x 50kg high explosive bombs and 60 incendiaries making a total of 2,000kg.

We left home with firstly the purpose of destroying the Waterworks at Hampton after gaining the necessary safe attack altitude and setting course for London itself.

At 7.35 p.m. the coast at Winterton was crossed and a course set for Cambridge. Until 8.30 p.m. the moon was shining, although its unfavourable light was dimmed somewhat by a layer of mist. Cambridge was easy to recognise as were other towns up to where the dim outline of London came into view.

Apart from ineffectual fire from the British guardships there was no real opposition until a gun near Enfield opened fire, this was directed with the help of searchlights, but soon two of these were extinguished and the fire silenced with the help of four of our HEs.

L13 then set course in a wide curve over Watford towards Kingston-upon-Thames which was located precisely from its characteristic position and we steered towards Hampton by following the curve of the Thames, confirming our course with the aid of light from flares, only one of which ignited properly although four were dropped.

We made three bombing runs, dropping in all, twelve high explosive bombs on the power-station and pumping house, although the darkness made it impossible to observe the extent of the damage.

After this we crossed London's southern suburbs and dropped the remainder of our bomb-load on the Victoria Docks. Gunfire defending the docks was very heavy compared with that experienced on the night of 8/9th October, and an improvement in the blackout was noticed.

Another surviving report accompanying that from Mathy is that from Alois Bocker, in command of L14 on the same night, which ran:

> On 13 October L14 received the order to take off on an attack against London, and this took place at 12.40 p.m. carrying 30 HE and 10 incendiary bombs.
>
> Shortly before reaching the English coast, which we crossed at Winterton at 7.20 p.m., we received heavy but ineffectual fire from the guardships, and later as we made our way towards London the ship was lit by the searchlights at Norwich, Thetford and Chelmsford and some anti-aircraft fire was encountered.
>
> At about 10 p.m. we saw another airship over London towards the West in process of dropping its bombs having crossed the Thames at Woolwich and we dropped nine High Explosive bombs on the Arsenal to good effect but in order to make an attack from the West, we first set a course South which brought us over Croydon a little after 11.30 p.m. where we dropped three explosive and ten incendiary bombs before steering a course over Battersea and Clapham where eighteen high explosive bombs were dropped. Many big fires and some large explosions were observed.
>
> While over London, L14 was lit bright as day by numerous searchlights, twenty-six being counted in all, and we were shot at from all sides by heavy fire, some of the shells exploding close to the vessel. On the outskirts of London, moreover, we encountered rockets which exploded high over our ship and more fire, although less heavy was encountered, accompanied by searchlights in the vicinities of Ipswich and Great Yarmouth, and it was at the latter that we finally crossed the coast at 2.50 a.m., setting course for Nordholz which we reached at 10.30 a.m. although a landing could not be made until 3.15 p.m. because of thick cloud.
>
> Examination of the ship revealed that it was undamaged.

The redoubtable Mathy, who gave the first account, had only about a year to live, being shot down by 2nd-Lt W.J. Tempest over Potters Bar on the night of 1 October 1916 while in command of L31, part of a force of eleven naval Zeppelins sent to attack targets in London and the Midlands. An eyewitness account of the event survives, coming from a lady who ran a dress shop which she had finally closed after a demanding day:

> I had been busy in the shop and was now going out to sweep the pavement. We screened all lights and stepped out, my mother and I, with our brushes. It was, I think after 12 o'clock, midnight; very dark, very quiet, there seemed to be no one about.
>
> We had been sweeping but a short time, when my mother touched my arm and pointed up at the sky, where there was something most awe-inspiring.
>
> A very long way off was what looked like a huge ship, very high up and smothered in flames, a really wonderful but frightening sight with the blaze all orange and yellow, blowing and billowing about, all the while slowly descending until at last it was out of sight.
>
> There was still no one about but us and I asked my mother if we ought to telephone the Police or Fire Station, but she assured me that it certainly hadn't gone unnoticed and in any case it must have been a long way off. 'God grant that there is nobody in whatever the object is' she said, and with sobering thoughts we went quietly to bed.

And thus Henrich Mathy died, along with his crew. He appeared to have jumped before his vessel hit the ground, judging from the imprint of the body deep in the turf, and he was technically alive when discovered, but died shortly afterwards. He seemed to have no injuries but reports mention a slight distortion of the face adding that he wore a muffler and heavy greatcoat over his uniform.

Greeted with jubilation in the newspapers, as were all reports of vanquished airships, Reverend Sandison had good reason to write to his brother shortly afterwards: 'It was about 12-something when Molly and I were awakened by, we knew not what. Probably the cheering down town, but Oh! these Zep nights. Another one down, so that I hear the people down town turned out into the streets and made a night of it cheering fiercely. Anyway the defence has scored, my idea being that we have airships of our own now and probably, not this one but the last that went down in flames fell to one or other and not to airoplanes [sic]'.

Some eighty years after the events, we know the reverend gentleman to be wrong, but the thoughts he expressed indicate that he was alive to the fact that the world was changing and the new arts of technology were even then affecting the way in which people lived – and fought each other. Most believed at the time that little or nothing was being done to combat enemy raiders over the Home Front, but Reverend Sandison was correct in his assumption, even if his facts were wrong; the problem was being addressed with some vigour, albeit cloaked in secrecy.

It was thanks to the new Munitions Inventions Department, created in August 1915 under the leadership of Captain E.W. Moir, then serving in the Royal Engineers, that a new range of innovative defence measures began to be trialled. Moir placed emphasis on researching early warning systems, concentrating particularly on ways of listening for the sound of airship motors. These were based on experience already gained from the use of 'listening wells' in France, excavations which presented a resonating surface to collect the sound waves, which were picked up and amplified with the aid of a sensitive microphone placed at their focal point – exactly the same principle as that which governs the operation of a satellite dish today. During testing this invention worked almost flawlessly, and this had been established quite early in the trials by using a tuning fork capable of simulating low-frequency sounds, such as those from an aero-motor. The system could even distinguish between an enemy or friendly aircraft motor. However, practical issues began to cloud theoretical considerations when problems arose from the fact that the wells tended to flood. There was a tentative decision to set up a trial system of such excavations spaced 2 miles (0.6km) apart, but by a process of logical thought it was not long before, with the aid of a parabolic reflector only some 4ft (1.21m) in diameter, it was decided to test the theory of a vertical reflector. This was 16ft (4.84m) in diameter, and cut in the chalk cliff at Binbury Manor, Kent, in the early summer of 1915. The prototype was tested with the aid of an unspecified RFC machine on 15 July of the same year, trials which soon led to the decision that improved echoes from sound mirrors faced with cement would be more effective since the surface was harder than natural chalk. Final reports indicated that an ideal mirror should be between an estimated 20 and 30ft (6.1 to 9.1m) in diameter, made on the spot from reinforced concrete and be mounted on gimbals to facilitate alignment of its 12 tons with the sound source.

Perhaps the best example of this new technology was the sound mirror (replaced by a 20ft, or 6.1m, vertical disc in the summer of 1918) at Joss Gap, near Broadstairs, reputedly capable of picking up the sound of an aero-engine at a distance of 50 miles (80km). Sound locators very similar in basic principle to these but of a reduced size and known as the MkIII model, were in use by the British Army in 1939, and were also used towards the closing years of the First World War as part of the assembly of searchlights and guns of the ground defences. These sound locators could be carried and assembled for use by a crew of four men, the official description of all three variants being 'of wood and metal construction, mounted on a stand'.

Considerably earlier than these developments, in about 1906, trials were being conducted to investigate the possibilities of wireless remote control of boats, torpedoes, airships and eventually aeroplanes, so that, in parallel with new methods of detection and improved standards of warning and interception, fresh methods of destroying 'aerial invaders', as raiders were described at one point, were investigated, quite apart from excursions into new fields of armament and ammunition.

The new fields of research were spearheaded by a number of organisations, including Sopwith and the Royal Aircraft Factory, who were becoming actively interested in the idea of remote control aircraft. ABC and Armstrong Siddeley were investigating the manufacture of specialist engines to power machines which were soon to be collectively known as 'aerial targets' (ATs) as a security cover, a name resulting from a plea from Sir David Henderson, Director-General of Military Aeronautics that 'a thundering great lie' must be invented to conceal the real purpose of these machines.

The idea of an unmanned, light, expendable aeroplane which would intercept enemy airships, wireless-controlled from the ground, was suggested towards the end of 1916, a year which was to see eighteen enemy airship attacks, and responsibility for design work was handed to the Royal Flying Corps Experimental Works, where 2nd-Lt (later Captain) Archibald M. Low RFC (later Professor A.M. Low) was currently working with a small team in a garage at Chiswick, attempting to evolve a suitable control system. Writing some forty years later he was to describe the frustrations of the work: 'No valves, only coherers were available [and] after many months of heartbreaking work largely connected with relays, and after we had tried every form of contact from platinum, gold and silver to iron, we produced a machine which more or less worked'. That this system seemed likely to be of use to guide the proposed AT meant orders to choose his own officers when 'the 'circus' was transferred to a hangar at Brooklands', and Low was allocated as assistants 'about thirty picked men, jewellers, carpenters and aircraftmen'. Everyone concerned was sworn to great secrecy and even their ranks and appointments were not gazetted in the usual way. Subsequent history recalls only the names of Captain Pool and Lieutenants Bowen and Whitton as among those involved.

Having produced a workable system which could also control the machine if it was packed with explosive and used as a flying bomb (when the operator would

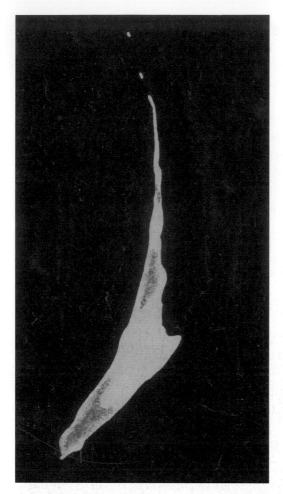

Alleged to be the last moments of Zeppelin L31 brought down on 1 October 1916 over Potters Bar by 2nd-Lt W. Tempest of No.39 Squadron. (Author's collection)

accompany the missile from a conventional aeroplane), the team was ordered to construct a suitable monoplane missile 'from tin and wood, using the wings from an old biplane'.

However, this work was not to meet with success, and the assistance of the Royal Aircraft Factory was sought, the actual evolution of a suitable type becoming the responsibility of Henry Folland assisted by H.E. Preston. The design which eventually emerged was a small, shoulder-wing monoplane with a simple skid undercarriage, powered by a 35hp horizontally opposed ABC Gnat motor which was the work of Granville Bradshaw, who attempted as far as possible to use low-grade materials since the motor was only intended for a working life of about two hours.

Flying controls were confined to those which actuated the rudder and elevators, a large dihedral angle to the wings ruling out the necessity for ailerons, wing-warping being employed instead, while limited engine control was also possible by radio from the operator on the ground, using a system of locks which could be re-set every morning. Stability of the missile was ensured by the use of an electrically driven gyro.

Low was later to write that the first proper flight was attempted on 12 March 1917, after the special unit had moved again, this time to Upavon. The first of six production machines arrived at Northolt on 5 June. Heavily guarded during preparations and overnight, trials were scheduled to commence on 6 July, before a gathering of senior officers.

When the great day arrived it was intended that first demonstration should be of the simplest nature, with the AT trimmed to take off and climb to a pre-determined altitude where wireless signals would take control, but alas, with the tailplane set at an angle of attack determined from the results of the then little-understood aerodynamic differences between the behaviour of scale models in a wing tunnel and full-size machines, and despite every detail being attended to, all did not go well.

Seen on the left, in 1916, eleven-year-old Marjorie Fowkes of Gretton. A contemporary of Madge Fowkes wrote the description of the Zeppelin incident reproduced here. (Courtesy Roger Fowkes)

The control lorry was driven smartly into position and the AT shot away with the assistance of compressed air, the planned procedure being that the missile would not be controlled from the lorry until it had reached sufficient height. Low, acting as an observer, was responsible for the actual working of the controls, under the direction of Major Henry Segrave, who was at that time an RFC officer and acting as 'pilot' of the craft. He was later to gain fame as a racing motorist with a knighthood.

The first command was a shout of 'up' and a hum of excitement was to be heard from the group of some thirty or forty generals. This was followed by the command 'left', and again 'up'. At this point Low happened to look over his shoulder, just in time to see the group of visitors running for their lives, creating a scene that has since passed into aviation folklore, with vivid descriptions of how the sudden eruption of activity to all points of the compass resembled the speedy opening of some exotic bloom, an illusion that was heightened, or so it has been alleged, by the fact that some of the senior officers were wearing the gorgeous uniforms of pre-war days! But however that may be, the first 'aerial target' ignominiously crashed only a few yards from the lorry, and in the following silence the voice of Major Gordon Bell – known at that time as 'the Mad Major', famed for his trenchant remarks as well as his stammer – loudly declared: 'I could throw my b-b-b-b-bloody umbrella further than that!'

The War Office was nevertheless anxious to give the projectile proper tests. However, when these were resumed on 25 July, the machine failed to take off, merely rushing about on the ground until brought to a halt when the undercarriage collapsed due to the tailplane adjustment now having been over-corrected. Another attempt three days later fared no better, crashing when the engine failed just after takeoff, and although the damage was minimal, being largely confined to a smashed undercarriage and broken airscrew, General Cadell's promising idea suggested two years earlier for a novel method of dealing with marauding airships was abandoned, very few understanding the description appended to the publication of the relevant patent in 1923 that it was for 'a rocket steered by radio to pursue enemy aircraft'.

The story of this abortive attempt to destroy airships during the war years gained a brief but not altogether irrelevant footnote in the early 1930s, when one of the surviving craft was converted by No.3 (Western) Aircraft Depot at Bristol for use as a small sports aircraft, fitted with ailerons and a wheeled undercarriage. By 1934 it had been disposed of by its owner to a Mr Ronald Shelly, a resident of Billericay. It was to be broken up not long after, without gaining a civilian identity.

Had these remotely-controlled defence weapons proved the success they were expected to be, the airship menace at which they were targeted could well have been defeated in a remarkably short time. As history shows us, however, the airships were to prevail, until they began to be replaced by aeroplanes in 1916. Thanks to advances made in the development of weight-carrying, extended-range, heavier-than-air craft, the planes slowly assumed the role of the vulnerable gas-bags. Even so, despite the name of the Gotha bomber replacing that of the Zeppelin in British conversation, the change was slow, as witness the following account penned by an eleven year old school girl, describing one of the enemy's last successful attacks in

Wearing patriotic ribbons in national colours enjoyed a brief fashion in 1914–15. These and the tassels on the right are in the shades of Belgium, France and Great Britain. (Author's collection)

1916; the Zeppelin responsible was the L34, the latest of the R-class vessels, which had only been commissioned about a week before and was commanded by Kplt Max Dietrich, and the district described is Gretton, near Kettering, Northants:

On Sunday night October the first the Zeppelins visited us. It was about 12 o'clock when they were first heard. It seemed they had lost their way and when they saw the woods they thought it was a town so they dropped some bombs. No one was hurt and only a few panes were blown out of the windows. Many bombs were dropped and most of them exploded. There were 42 bombs dropped. The smell of the engines was awful.

When they were first heard they were over Harringworth Woods, they came zig-zag to Dudley's field along the Weldon Road and dropped four bombs in it. They then came across the fields to the Lodges and dropped more bombs. Then they went across to the tunnel and when the gun at Corby started firing they turned back and went over Uppingham.[*]

---

[*] This was sited on high ground above the village, as it had been discovered that, if fired on, enemy airships tended to drop their bomb-loads and turn for home. This led to many anti-aircraft guns being situated on the flight-paths to large cities. Seemingly this is what took place in this case.

THREE

A CHANGING WORLD

Undoubtedly the most seismic changes that war was to bring were those that began to take place in the period immediately following the official declaration of war. In those first few days, anyone travelling to the bank found that it was not open (a wise official precaution to prevent a rush on withdrawals). People spontaneously began to stockpile food. Another major change was the immediate call-up of service reservists, their first duty being a call at the Post Office to claim the official train fare of three shillings (15p) for travel to their designated enlistment centre.

In the atmosphere of change and adaptation, the War Office was swift to act, commandeering mental asylums in order to use them as ordinary hospitals. Even the new wing of the grandstand on Epsom Downs was taken over for this purpose, with the result that the last race for the duration of the war was held in the spring of the following year. The only spectators, however, were patients fortunate enough not to be confined to a bed. Later, casualties arrived here in great numbers from the abortive assault on Gallipoli. Among these were Australians and New Zealanders wounded by Turkish fire, as well as those struck down by dysentery and typhoid.

The role of the Boy Scouts was to undergo extensive change, as they were given responsibility for many important wartime tasks. One of the jobs the Scouts were given was the sounding of civilian signals to indicate that enemy raiders had passed. This task they shared with the Church Lads' Brigade, and it is touched on elsewhere in this work, but the further responsibilities of the Scouts were to prove much wider.

In their local areas, these tasks were to include the picketing of railway stations and bridges, a task that was among the earliest of their commitments, their war service being accepted only six years after their foundation by Sir Robert Baden-Powell, the hero of Mafeking, the town long besieged in the South African War

An officer of the Church Lads' Brigade, another youth organisation which made numerous contibutions to civilian life in some districts during 1914–1918. (N.W. Cruwys' collection)

between October 1899 and May of the following year. Other local activities after the outbreak of war included acting as messengers, in some districts especially to assist the YMCA, as well as collecting clean re-usable wood for the Hospital Woodwork Depots and clean waste paper for the National Relief Fund. The Scouts also acted as guides for troops newly posted to an area with which they were unfamiliar.

Other duties more obviously connected with the war included regularly assisting in servicemen's canteens and recreation centres, fatigue work in hospitals, collecting money towards the purchase of motor-ambulances for use in France, as well as regularly collecting for such charities as Dr Barnardo's, this being a time at which the charity's funds were at a low due to wartime conditions.

But if one is tempted to give an indulgent or amused smile to war-work of this nature, it should be remembered that although the structure of the fellowship meant that the boys were generally given tasks with which they were familiar, some went further afield to serve their country. Perhaps the best example of this is the fact that some sought employment as Coast Watchers. There was one group from Surrey, standing in while volunteers were found from five troops in Kent,

CLB colours are trooped at a camp just before the outbreak of hostilities. (N.W. Cruwys' collection)

assigned to patrol the 45 miles of coast between Pegwell Bay and Dungeness on bicycles, as early as August 1914. They maintained this vigil until local Scouts could take over. Another troop found themselves assisting with military transport at Newhaven, about 100 miles from their home area, for a protracted period between October 1914 and the following January. Others carried out similar work at Littlehampton for almost a year until the beginning of 1916.

All this coastal patrol work was carried out under the supervision of the local Coastguards during the hours of darkness. Daylight hours saw the boys performing standard look-out duties, so occasions when they were called on to help with beaching, launching, mooring and towing the nearby RNAS seaplanes, must have come as an interesting diversion. They were highly regarded in this work; as a result of an incident, the details of which are now lost, Flight Commander F.J. Bailey wrote to the boys thanking them for their 'invaluable service in saving his machine'. This is high commendation for a comparatively small group of boys, less than twenty in number, who found no problem in being accommodated at the time in a Coastguard cottage where they were responsible for their own messing, cooking and washing.

Above left: Sea Scout keeps watch on the part of the South Coast it is his responsibility to patrol. (Courtesy Boy Scouts Association)

Above right: Sea Scout checking passes before allowing entrance to a sensitive area. (Courtesy Boy Scouts Association)

It is not widely realised that the employment of citizens sworn in to assist the regular police in times of emergency is a result of the riots provoked by the passing of the Reform Bill in the nineteenth century. Those riots resulted in the Special Constables Act of 1831, 'Specials' being used to quell those riots as well as the later Chartist riots, which did not die out until 1849. With the outbreak of the First World War, a nationwide appeal resulted in attested men reporting for duty as early as the fourth week in August 1914.

It had been correctly anticipated that the strength of the regular constabulary would be reduced due to men volunteering for the Forces, but when military service was made compulsory, a move unforeseen at the outbreak of war, police strength was weakened even further, at a time when the demands on the regulars were greatly increased.

The creation of a trained rescue service similar to that planned and implemented before 1939 was hardly even contemplated in 1914, the chances of air attacks on the British Isles being regarded as remote. Ultimately, therefore, such work fell to the fire brigades and police.

Included in the wartime duties of both Specials and Regulars was the guarding of 'vulnerable points' – locations regarded as being at risk from saboteurs, including waterworks, reservoirs, pumping stations, telephone exchanges, subways, gas and electricity stations, railway junctions and bridges. However, most were only guarded for a brief time between 21 September and 9 October 1914, when protection was withdrawn from all sites except selected gas and electricity works, pumping stations and telephone exchanges. In general terms, these continued to be protected until the middle of June 1917, with guarding of some telephone exchanges and main waterworks continuing until early November 1917, when it was withdrawn in the London area.

These duties are of historical interest as the only recorded use up until that point of British police regularly carrying firearms. This was all work which increased the load on the police considerably, since 'Lighting Orders' had to be enforced and 'specials' were now about to be employed in laying the foundations of the Metropolitan Observation Service, later to become the Observer Corps, as detailed in another chapter. The war had also ushered in many other new responsibilities, such as finding billets for troops and keeping the roads open for military convoys.

Boy Scout buglers were responsible for sounding the 'All Clear' for an area. (Author's collection)

Surviving Boy Scout cloth badges.

Top left: Coast Watching, eighty-four days. *Right*: One year. There were also similar badges for two and three years with appropriate number of rings.

Centre: General, twenty-eight days' service and fifty days. Similar Wolf Cub badges existed for twenty-eight and fifty days' service with a circular one for 100 days. All red on gold.

Below: General War Service badges for 100 and 1,200 days' service. There were also similar badges for 300, 600 and 900 days' service with the appropriate number of outer rings, each representing 300 days' service. All were gold on a red background. (Courtesy Boy Scouts Association)

Our Canteen and Post Office, Roffey.

The Young Men's Christian Association, which had only recently adopted the triangular logo at this time provided a welcome sight of civilised behavior for weary soldiers on leave. (Author's collection)

In some areas, a car or even a small number of cars were at the disposal of Special Constables carrying out normal police work, the organisational system often involving a number of assembly centres, these being located so that men could operate from them in such a manner that an entire town was 'covered'. It was to these centres that the men reported on the first intimation of a 'call' (a report of a likely air raid) and placed on 'standby' duty in groups of nine under the command of a Sergeant. These centres, which were in touch with each other and Police Headquarters by telephone, also acted as assembly points for members of the Red Cross, St John's Ambulance drivers and VAD (Voluntary Aid Detachment) nurses. Simultaneously, a 'call' would see constables dispatched to standby at street fire alarms.

A local force of Specials often included an Ambulance Section equipped with a motor vehicle and wheeled stretcher, those manning this section being holders of First Aid Certificates. Additionally some of the men serving as Specials were graded as Buglers in order to augment the Boy Scouts and members of the Church Lads Brigade to sound the 'all-clear' at the end of an attack.

Uniform of even the simplest type for members of the Specials was in some areas slow to be issued, the first members carrying out their duties in their private clothes with merely a lapel badge or brassard for identification, but by 1917 most had peaked caps and a mackintosh. London did rather better, even before the issue of caps in 1915; members who paraded in civilian dress did so with armlets indicating rank, those of Inspectors being blue, Sub-Inspectors being red, and Sergeants, yellow. At the end of the same year boots and overcoats were available

This was the cover of a booklet recording the work of the Metropolitan Observation Service issued privately to former members in early 1919. (Derek Wood collection)

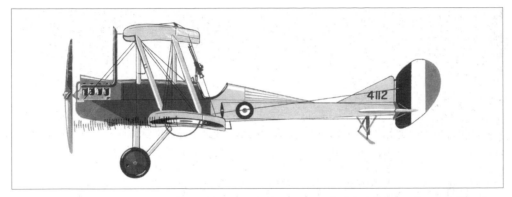

Above: Most used among British aircraft for intercepting raiders were the BE2 types. This Bristol-built BE2c was flown as a single-seater by Lt Sowrey to destroy L32 on the night of 23 September 1916. (Author)

Right: These nurses from Ivy Lodge Stoke Park, Stapleton in 1913 would have been typical of those who went to war fifteen months later. (Author's collection)

for every man. In May 1916 full uniforms were provided, the coloured armlets now being no longer necessary since normal rank insignia was worn. However, some county forces had to wait until the spring of 1917 before being provided with any type of uniform, and even this sometimes amounted only to a badge, cap and waterproof.

It was not until six months after the Armistice that Britain's Specials were finally disbanded, on 16 June 1919. A Special Constabulary Medal was struck for those who had served for three years or more, Special Stars going to men who had joined the force in 1914. Their work had been variable and demanding, including not only the more prosaic roles described earlier, but more intriguing duties such as keeping order at London Underground stations (see chapter five), security work at the opening of Parliament, carrying out patrols to maintain the safety of foreign nationals during the outbreak of anti-German riots in the spring of 1915, and rounding up deserters from the armed forces.

Another change wrought by war was that the Home Office now took responsibility for co-ordinating the activities of Chief Constables, supplying a measure of leadership which was to last into the post-war world, and which was to result in closer operational collaboration.

In addition to the Special Constabulary there also existed in 1914 a force of some 4,000 men who were retained as a police reserve and paid a retaining fee, but in practice this total was rapidly reduced to something like half its initial number, mainly due to its pensioner members succumbing to the strenuous physical demands of police work.

There is no doubt that the First World War was a severely testing time for both the regular constabulary and the Specials, the latter being neither exceptionally popular with their professional colleagues nor among the inhabitants of the poorer districts who regarded them with a deep hatred. Additionally, police morale left something to be desired, the root cause being the insult of a parsimonious pay structure allied to draconian discipline, an example of which had occurred in 1909, with the dismissal of an inspector for 'undue familiarity with his men'. It was as a result of this low morale, compounded in 1918 after a massive quantity of overtime, much of it the result of cancelled leave, remained unpaid, that a police strike began on 30 August 1918. However, this was short-lived as, on the following day, the men's delegates having met General Smutts and Prime Minister Lloyd George, the pair, perhaps feeling guilty, conceded to the demands made, and normal duties were resumed with an air of triumph.

As an era drew on, a sign of how domestic life was changing forever was the slow disappearance of horse-drawn vehicles from the streets. On Wednesday 25 October 1911, the last horse-bus departed from London Bridge Station, a vehicle that was for so long a part of the history of a London of Hansom cabs, 'Growlers' and horse-trams, all of which would last only a few years longer in an England where a schoolboy[*] of 1912 carried for the rest of his life a memory of the Aerial Derbys of 1911 and 1912, with the confidence of youth believing that motors were no more than a novelty. Indeed, it is true that they were little more than a plaything for a group of Cambridge undergraduates who organised a race through the town's narrow streets in reverse at some time before the First World War.

Nevertheless, that the universal use of horses would eventually give way to mechanical transport was nowhere more clearly evident than in the London Fire Brigade, which at the time of the First World War was engaged in a programme of replacing horse-drawn appliances with motorised vehicles, capable of maintaining a speed of 32mph! On the other hand, strangely, the Metropolitan Police, in an emergency document of 1910, which outlined policies to be introduced in the event of war, made provision for the requisitioning of horses. Although this was never implemented, it is not widely realised how reliant the armies of many nations were on horses in the opening years of the new twentieth century, these animals being known as 'remounts' in England, a term applied irrespective of whether they were draft animals, cavalry horses or officers' chargers.

---

[*] Later group captain Peter Wright, who was to command No.114 Squadron, RAF, flying Bristol Blenheims from Nantes until ordered to evacuate and leave France in May 1940.

It was as early as August 1914 when the War Office appointed Reginald Sherriff Summerhays, one of the most knowledgeable men in equine matters then living, as a Civilian Remount Purchasing Officer. His role was to tour the country, along with his representatives, securing suitable animals. One lady recalls how a farmer at Chipstead, Surrey, wept like a child as his horses, chosen as suitable for hauling guns, were taken out of the gate for the last time. 'They never came back', she added. This was just one of the 4,000,000 lost.

While demands such as these brought sadness to some, it brought opportunity to others, a typical example being the newspaper advertisement which appeared in September 1914, enquiring:

Have any of YOUR horses or vans been Commandeered? We can Supply You with MOTOR VANS on very Reasonable Terms – The Connaught Motor & Carriage Company Co. Ltd, 27-29 Long Acre, London, WC.

The use of obedient animals in the horrors of war is repugnant to any nation which claims to be civilised and, as tales reached those at home of the sufferings of horses and other animals, there was a swift response, the nation seeing the establishment of several specialist charities aimed at alleviating the suffering of animals in war. Typical were the reports that emerged from Arras in the spring of 1917 telling how, when Royal Horse Artillery drivers attempted to take the girths and back-packs off their animal, the harness, having been so long in place, stripped the animal's flesh away. More than one young infantryman, newly arrived at the Front, was to discover that the first duty he would perform was burying a dead horse.

However, there were other, less unpleasant, tales to be told concerning animals, one being the case of the officer on the Somme who came into a base camp one morning and asked 'Does anyone here know anything about horses?' A young man replied 'Yes sir', pausing in his tuneful rendition of a Salvationist hymn, 'I do. I was a groom before I was called up!' 'Then you can look after my horse', the officer replied, and this the man did for the remainder of the war. He returned unscathed, adding to the author 'If it hadn't been for my officer and that horse, I'd probably have ended up as cannon-fodder!'

Conversely, while the Army was searching far and wide for suitable horses, at much the same time the more efficient fire brigades at home were re-equipping where finance permitted with motor appliances, although the exigencies of war were to prevent this completely, even some parts of London until 1921, despite the original plan to phase out horses being scheduled for completion in 1914.

This goal had already been achieved at some fire stations, such as that covering London's Soho which had lost all its horses at the beginning of that year. Yet, an illustration of how severely the programme was affected by wider events is indicated by a report on a call to the Enfield Brigade to douse the flames of the Schutte-Lanz SL11 airship, brought down at Cuffley on 3 September 1916. The report relates how 'the horses arrived the next morning steaming from the race up the hill', and still, on 7 July in the following year, when the Central Telegraph Office was set alight by enemy action, at least one team arrived drawn by a pair of the London Brigade's traditional percherons, a breed combining strength with speed, their appliance being one capable of pumping some 300 gallons of water per minute in a jet reaching a height of almost 160ft at a pressure of about 150psi.

Foremost among the new era of motorised fire appliances was that which heralded the entry in 1908 of Dennis Brothers of Guildford, Surrey, to a new market. The makers described their invention as a 'motorised, self-propelled vehicle', capable of carrying a wheeled escape. This was in all probability the well-known Bailey design of the period, the escape of which was capable of being extended to a length of 47ft 6in, the height of an average fifth-floor window, while the Dennis machine's pump was capable of delivering a jet at a pressure of 1,000psi. The cost of this appliance was £2,200 and although hard-tyred, the makers claimed it could reach a speed of 38mph. Development of this appliance was continuous, reaching its zenith in the 1914 model.

However, the first British self-propelled petrol motor fire engine in use by a public fire brigade was that delivered to Finchley Fire Brigade on 23 November 1904, designed by Merryweather & Sons. This was capable of carrying a 50ft wheeled escape in addition to a sixty gallon soda-acid tank under the driver's seat for immediate use until the main pump could be started. A new, more powerful motor was fitted to this appliance in 1912 and, since it remained in use until 1928, it naturally follows that it saw service during the First World War.

A natural consequence of the gradual adoption of motorised fire engines was that the traditional means of clearing the way for an appliance speeding to answer a call, in London by means of the entire crew shouting a chant of 'Hi, Yi', was no longer practical. Bells were introduced, although this method of warning had been anticipated by the Bristol Police Fire Brigade, this force having fitted an automatic gong under the driver's foot-board, was activated by a pedal above, which was used in the horse-drawn 'chemical engine' (once again using the bicarbonate of soda-sulphuric acid principle) which was in use between 1902 and 1914. Carrying thirty-five gallons of water, 150ft of ¾ in hose and ladder sections capable of being assembled to a length of 40ft.

A small number of fire brigades prior to the outbreak of war in 1914 were also adding to their fleet a new concept. Designed in 1908 and marketed at £122, they were known as 'First Aid Fire Cars', being in all essentials a two-man motor tricycle with a locker in front. This contained hoses, rescue equipment, fire extinguishers and a folding ladder, its purpose being to precede the main appliance to a fire, which would still have been preparing to set off, or would be getting horsed-up.

Equipment for fire-fighting had also been improved in several other areas by the outbreak of war, 1906 seeing the introduction of the first turn-table ladders which could be turned through 360 degrees and, being metal, could be extended to a height of 82ft. They were also capable of being fitted to horse-drawn articulated vehicles. Trials of breathing apparatus also began at about the same time.

Yet although technological advances were being made in fire-fighting, relations between the firemen and their officers were not always as promising. The period before 1914 was an especially unhappy time, particularly in London where the men were becoming increasingly discontented and officers are said to have found difficulty in maintaining discipline in the capital. The strength here totalled only 1,250 men and this number was reduced by 280 as Army and Navy reservists in the force responded to call for men to join the armed forces. Surprisingly, little or nothing was done to halt this. The London County Council agreed that the families of these men would not be evicted from their quarters, and a further 140 soon followed for the same reason, the result of all this being that some ten weeks after the outbreak of war, the total strength of London's brigade was reduced to about 850 men, a crisis which the LCC announced its intention to tackle by cancelling the proposal that men would be allowed one day off per week instead of the standard one day free per fortnight.

War also brought about a number of changes in the demands made on fire brigades and, although there were of course still many fires unrelated to enemy attacks, such as the blaze which occurred on a Sunday night in June 1915 when a fire in a copra store at Regent's Canal Dock did damage to the value of £14,000, the new workload caused by enemy bombs, and also crashed aircraft, placed unprecedented strain on the early twentieth-century brigades. Incidents involving downed planes were particularly problematic, as they could quickly spread petrol along busy city streets, with streams of the liquid running along the tram tracks, or setting alight tarred road blocks.

The lack of adequate preparation in these areas was the result of the comfortable assumption, mentioned earlier, that there would be no significant airship attacks on Britain. Some in government firmly assured themselves that enemy airships could not fly in the dark, while daylight appearances would be quickly and efficiently dealt with by the defences – a strange, blinkered attitude in view of the horror with which the wider public faced the possibility of such raids. As if to gain confirmation that this attitude should be adopted, Lord Kitchener was consulted by the LCC, only for the council to receive an unexpected rebuke from the Secretary for War, who stated that firemen served their country no less than men at the Front. There was a note of panic in the LCC's subsequent announcement that sappers, the Salvage Corps or private brigades could always be relied upon to assist at fires. However, when an official application for firemen to be granted exemption from military service was refused, a ridiculous 'remedy' was proposed, whereby the 2,000 postmen who had been granted exemption could be used. Their total lack of training was conveniently ignored.

There was only one answer to this problem, and it came in 1915, when exemption from service in the armed forces was at last granted to fire fighters. Just as swiftly, however, this was withdrawn, and then again restored with some haste after serious enemy attacks on London in 1917. Following these raids, it was announced that experienced firemen were to be recalled from service with the colours abroad. Indeed, the realisation that the British Isles were little more than a lightly protected target seemed to dawn on the authorities quite suddenly and by October 1916 enquiries were coming from the War Office, asking if any of the smaller local fire brigades were prepared to sell any Merryweather or Shand Mason horse-drawn fire engines. The request stimulated some of the lesser, local fire committees to upgrade their equipment, since it was to prove possible to dispose of a Dennis pump-tender with a light 3ft ladder, with a 40 gallon tank and pump capable of delivering water at 250-300 gallons per minute for £1,038. Old (c.1885) Shand Mason horse-drawn engines fetched rather less, at about £100.

It was less than a year later, on 25 September 1917, that, under the ubiquitous Defence of the Realm Act (DORA) the many local fire brigades (around 90 in number) within the 750sq. miles of the London area were co-ordinated. This did not approach the scale of the National Fire Service, set up in the Second World War, but took the form of a system whereby on the receipt of warning of a potential attack, a minimum of nine motor fire appliances from outside brigades were expected to assemble at a pre-determined rendezvous and await orders, while others were placed on standby. This was regarded as Phase One; Phase Two was a call for a greater concentration of equipment, both motorised and horse-drawn to close in and standby. Phase One was activated nineteen times, Phase Two only once.

That such measures were possible was due to two factors, one being that the manpower shortage had by now forced some of the smaller, local fire brigades to close their regional fire stations, and the second being the state of the roads of the time, in outlying areas often little more that tracks which forced only slow speeds on drivers.

In addition to these consolidation measures, all fire stations were now linked by emergency telephones which created a network to which ammunition factories and service bases in the Metropolitan area had access.

Ammunition factories obviously constituted the greater risk and therefore had most need of contact with fire brigades, a large number of these factories having sprung up in a short space of time all over the country. Even the smaller works had a large output; a factory in a motor workshop was recorded as producing a grand total of 250,000 shells, while another, smaller, engineering works achieved an output of 103,621. Smaller still, the grand total manufactured by a gas and water undertaking was proudly announced to be 21,630.

Perhaps the largest fire which the London Brigade had to tackle was not caused by enemy action, although it could certainly be blamed on the war. This took place in January 1917, beginning as a small fire in the huge munitions factory at Silvertown, West Ham in east London, adjoining the Royal Victoria Dock. This was already being tackled by a detachment of the local brigade when, a little before 7 p.m., a huge explosion took place, destroying the appliance, killing a sub-officer and a fireman and blowing in the windows of the fire station, which was only a few yards away, as well as killing two children in the living quarters. The force of the explosion was such that windows were blown in on the opposite side of the river at Blackheath, a total of sixty-nine people being killed, twenty-six of them women and children, plus 400 injured.

These casualties were, however, 'light', as there were at the time no workers inside the factory buildings. As it was, a gas holder with a capacity of 9,000,000 cubic feet of coal gas formed a separate inferno, the sparks blowing across the river and starting a new fire at Greenwich in the yard of a tar manufacturer.

Obviously a conflagration of these dimensions was too much for the East Ham men, and a call for assistance was made to the London Fire Brigade which, despite already having to fight the blazes on their own side of the Thames, immediately sent two fire boats and twenty-nine motor pumps to create a combined force which was in attendance at Silvertown for ten days.

By comparison, many of the fires which had to be fought as the result of bombing attacks were of lesser magnitude, although serious enough in their own right, such as those of 31 May 1915, when a bomb, seemingly one of the ninety incendiaries dropped by LZ38 on the Stoke Newington area of London forty minutes before midnight, started a massive fire which reportedly brought about the deaths of six of the seven people killed that night, as well as triggering a serious outbreak of rioting, targeting persons and property of assumed German origin. This raid, in which LZ38 was accompanied by LZ37, was that which marked the Kaiser's reluctant agreement to allow attacks on districts of London which lay east of the Tower. The shell of one of the incendiaries dropped that night has been preserved to this day.

Another serious raid was that of 8-9 September in the same year, in which L13, accompanied by L14 and the short-range L9, which bombed Skimingrove, targeted Golders Green, going on to scatter a number of high explosive bombs,

Two oil bombs now preserved in Northampton, that on the left having been dropped on 1 October 1916 at Gratton, and that on the right on Islip Parish on 31 January/1 February 1918. (Courtesy Northampton Museums)

including one of 660lb, along the railway line from Euston to Liverpool Street. Reports were heavily censored, as it was feared that news that twenty-five motor pumps had been necessary to deal with the resultant blazes, one in which a fireman had died, would create fresh outbreaks of panic among the population.

But there were other dangerous, if smaller, responsibilities for the firemen of the First World War. These included dealing with aircraft crashes and, following a bombing attack, rescuing survivors, there being no separate rescue service as in the Second World War, with the police, fire brigades and the Army's Pioneer Corps expected to perform these tasks. In return for all this, an individual man's pay was 2s 6d (13p) for the first hour's attendance at an incident, and 1s 6d (8p) per hour thereafter, with special rates for prolonged duties. These were sums paid over and above a weekly salary of perhaps 26s 6d (£1.30), with an additional 2s 6d (13p) for those men living off-station, a sum doubled in Hampshire in January 1917, although the widow of a man who had served for twenty years could expect a gratuity of just £25.

The smaller brigades were more cheaply maintained, one being described in January 1916 as consisting of 'twenty-two men and three officers, with two old men doing duty'. But in other spheres, the war brought unexpected work to the fire brigades, the calls on a Chief Officer's time now including giving advice on fire precautions at military hospitals and convalescent homes, in addition to sitting on innumerable committees, including those which enforced lighting regulations.

Just as the work of the trained Rescue Squads of the Second World War was anticipated in the First World War by the police, fire brigades and Pioneers, there were also none of the designated Air-Raid Wardens, so crucial during the Blitz, to assist during the Zeppelin raids. Instead very similar work was carried out on a self-regulatory basis by volunteers, chiefly in London's northern and eastern parishes. They called themselves 'patrols', and their houses were identified by a large letter 'P' prominently displayed in a window.

The aim of these 'patrols' was primarily to put a stop to local outbreaks of panic following false alarms, as is made clear in the recollections of a writer of the period:

> As soon as everything was quiet and the people settled down for the night, there came to opportunity for the false alarmist. He would break in on one's first slumberings, rousing the whole neighbourhood, and by his precipitate haste and wild shrieks create a dismal panic where no panic was.

Another describes the panic created by cries of 'Take cover, take cover. A terrible attack from the air is coming!' The 'patrols', more responsibly, woke any who wished to be disturbed after the likelihood of a raid had been confirmed by the local police station, and later some districts had arrangement with the police whereby notices of impeding raids were sent to patrol centres. With a large number of their 'customers', that is, those who specified that they wished to be woken, being engaged in war work, raising them from their slumbers after a day in a factory was sometimes a lengthy business, and so occasionally attacks on doors with wooden potato mashers were necessary to rouse them.

Patrol organisation was efficient, with local reporting points often being set up in parish rooms; the associated clergy, some of whom were ordinary patrol members as well, might double as group chairmen, and in one district alone the total patrol strength had risen to 300 men over a period of two years, these being divided for operational purposes into 'sections', each under an appointed Sergeant, who in turn worked under the supervision of a Patrol Inspector. Peabody Buildings in East London had its own team of patrols, and a meeting place within the block dedicated by the Trustees. Local reporting points were regularly staffed on a nightly basis by two men between 10 p.m. and 2 a.m., no small self-sacrifice since many of the members had to be at work only four hours later. Others kept watch between 10 p.m. and 4 a.m. or 11 p.m. to 5.30 a.m., the variable times being arranged according to the season and length of daylight hours.

Some 'patrol bands', as one contemporary writer terms them, had the advantage of a properly equipped ambulance section with such apparatus as a wheeled mobile stretcher, together with four others of the usual kind, plus a comprehensive first-aid kit. Typical of the work undertaken was that to which a 'section' with these facilities was directed in North East London, where a house had received very severe damage in a raid, firemen having extracted a woman and small boy, both gravely injured. Although both were rushed to hospital by the crew of the ambulance section, the lady subsequently died. It was agreed, however, that the life of the child had been saved by the patrol's prompt action.

Although the Boy Scouts are best-remembered for their sounding of the 'All Clear' they were joined in some districts by the Boy's Brigade. This figure at the entrance to a church hall shows their uniform. (Author)

Belgian refugees pose in their best outfits. (Author's collection)

The lucky Belgians escaped as complete family units, illustrated here by this couple and their three children. (Courtesy Roger Fowkes)

Left: Belgian servicemen such as this unnamed soldier also found temporary lodging in Britain during the early days of the conflict. (Courtesy Roger Fowkes)

Below: Some refugees filled in their time with raising money for charity. This model aeroplane was constructed from a cork, feathers, leaves and shirt buttons by Lt Charles Alyier of the Regiment de Carabiniers and the Belgian Flying Corps who was wounded at Dixmude. (Courtesy Bexhill Costume Museum)

MODEL OF AN AEROPLAN

Built out of Tree Leaves, an Acorn, a Match, and Shirt Buttons, by

Charles Alyier
1 regiment de carabinier
Wounded at Diesmude

BELGIAN AVIATOR CORPS.

Working in conjunction with these there often existed Divisions of the St John's Ambulance Brigade, one of which, operating in the part of the capital which lies between Moorgate and London Wall, raised a total of £250, a substantial sum in those days, with which to purchase a motor ambulance for its area which was served by no less than thirty nurses.

Patrols operating in the large complex building blocks that had been erected in the East End had a particularly difficult task during air raids, since the only public shelters were those in the Underground stations, Patrol members had evolved the strategy of assembling women and children on a first-floor landing of such buildings, it being believed that the three concrete floors above them would give sufficient protection in the event of all but a direct hit. Other work undertaken by patrols included the maintenance of a watching brief on the sale and supply of foodstuffs in the locality and on the distribution of coal, with particular attention to its supply to the elderly and those women whose men were away. Later, new members of the organisation were enrolled as sub-Specials in the Metropolitan Police. These men, of which there were 200, wore a distinctive badge, and a pair were expected to stay up all night in rotation, to keep order in public shelters, this being the chief responsibility of sub-Specials.

One problem encountered by patrols, police and other public service workers was that of language. There were large numbers of residents that had settled from abroad and, living in districts mostly populated by others of their own nationality, they knew little of other tongues. An illustration of this was the parish with a population of 25,000, of whom some 21,000 were Jewish immigrants, in the main from Belgium, Germany, Holland and Romania. It was the opinion of the area's British minority that the majority of these immigrants were of a naturally timorous disposition, this being, according to one contemporary source, the result of 'the harsh treatment which has been their lot for the last 2,000 years from almost every nation'. Later, the reporter went on to give a word-picture of the behaviour of these people when an enemy attack was expected:

> At the least hint of a raid, even in the most impossible weather for such ventures, the streets are full of hurrying crowds, eager to get to the nearest shelter. Old crones are dragged through the streets, urged to greater speed by the beseechings of sons, daughters and grandchildren, with fathers, mothers, babies galore, children of every age – all burdened with chairs, boxes, coats, wraps and baskets of food – all running for safety. Efforts to reason with them are for the most part, fruitless… I have been out at all hours, sometimes between 2 and 3 a.m., endeavouring to stop a rush from a purely imaginary danger.

The war brought about many changes, and it is often overlooked quite how many of these continued into the subsequent interwar years. Postmen were allowed to practice regularly with smallbore rifles all the way up to the early 1930s, the issue of identity cards in 1939 was based on a similar scheme around 1919, and even the re-establishment of the Women's Land Army, first introduced with the opening of a recruitment drive in the spring of 1917, created a workforce which did not officially end its existence until November two years later. Additionally, records exist proving that between December 1914 and June 1919, the war spawned no less than nineteen new public flag days, two of the earliest being those making charitable collections for Serbians, these being swiftly followed by collections for Russia and Belgium.

So much had changed, and continued to do so, in the everyday lives of the British public, that to the thinking man and woman it became clear that any chance of a hoped-for return to the 'old days' of imagined happiness and tranquillity was fading. Changes were everywhere, including such small changes as the sacrifice of a former custom by postmen, who always announced their delivery by a vigorous attack on the knocker. Among some of the older men, at least, this was to survive into the Second World War. Girls acting as conductors on buses and trams were still fresh in the memory twenty years later as the prevailing norm, as was the memory of Sally Holmes the conductoress of one of Sunderland's trams who was wounded while on duty, said to have been the very first 'clippie' to be struck down at her work.

FOUR

SOUND AN ALARM

Paranoia gripped Great Britain, largely generated by the understandable German pride in having won the current arms race, but also exploited by Germany's propagandists and accentuated by journalists in England who, having earlier gained a reputation for accuracy and sound judgement, quickly sacrificed their standards and made for quick returns by trading in sensationalism and public alarm. However, it was soon clear from the enemy incursions into English air space from the earliest days of the war, that the country was now faced with a problem never before encountered, and measures to meet this threat were called for urgently.

It fell to Major (later Lieutenant Colonel, CMG, DSO) R.E.H. James of MT2 (Directorate of Military Training) at the War Office to address the problem late in 1914, one of his suggestions being an ambitious plan for two lines of observation posts, 10 miles apart, running from the English Channel to the river Tweed, the outer line set roughly 20 miles inland and individual posts at 10 to 15 miles from each other.

This idea was never to be realised, and instead, in an area 60 miles round London, police officers on their beat were expected to stay alert for any sign of airships, and immediately telephone any sightings to the Admiralty, which was at that time still acting in its traditional role of nation's guardian. The Admiralty would, in turn, inform the War Office, Scotland Yard and various railway companies.

In sparsely populated areas, meanwhile, the people were urged to keep a wary eye and a sharp ear, and to telephone any suspicions to the authorities. Somewhat complex notices detailing the procedure ran thus:

> If you see an airship or aeroplane try and note these points about her. Then as quickly as possible, call up 'Anti-aircraft, London' on the nearest telephone. Commence your message with the words 'Aircraft Report' and proceed to give your information in the following order...

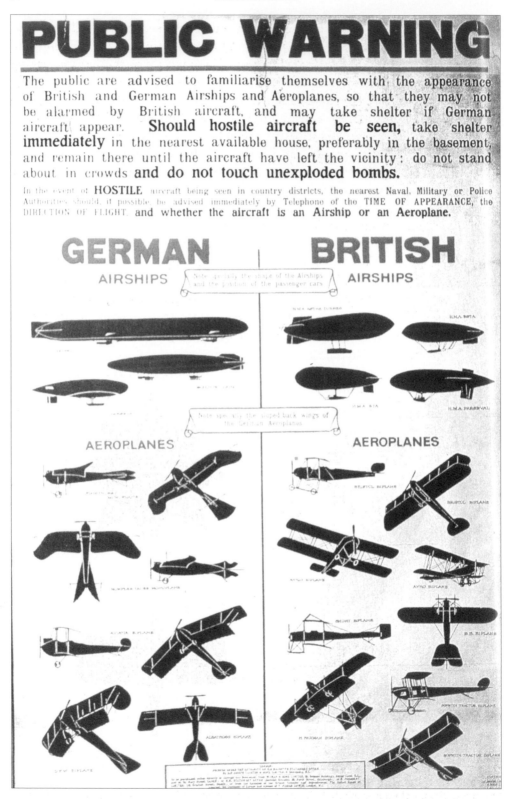

Public Warning poster showing comparative silhouettes of enemy and allied aircraft in 1915. (IWM)

Members of the public were expected to distinguish between airship and aeroplane, and also give approximate location of the sighting, the time of the sighting, and the direction in which the craft was heading. The identity of the person making the report was required, as was information regarding the volume of the aircraft's engines, its colour and markings. If it was an aeroplane, the authorities wanted to know whether it was a biplane or monoplane, and whether it had any lettering. If an airship, how many cars did it have? A telephone number was appended.

By the following year it was clear that the early hopes of a speedy victory were not to be realised, January seeing enemy airship attacks on targets at Yarmouth, King's Lynn and even London itself four months later, so that the system of reporting aerial incursions was extended to cover East Anglia, Nottinghamshire, Oxfordshire, Hampshire and the Isle of Wight.

By April, the War Office began to show an increased interest in the reporting system, perhaps as a result of an M-class Zeppelin having successfully penetrated to within 90 miles of the English coast, clearly bound for the Thames Estuary despite the prevailing dark and squally conditions, before having to turn back due to engine trouble. Chief Constables were now ordered to inform the Army authorities of potential air attacks as well as liaising with neighbouring constabularies.

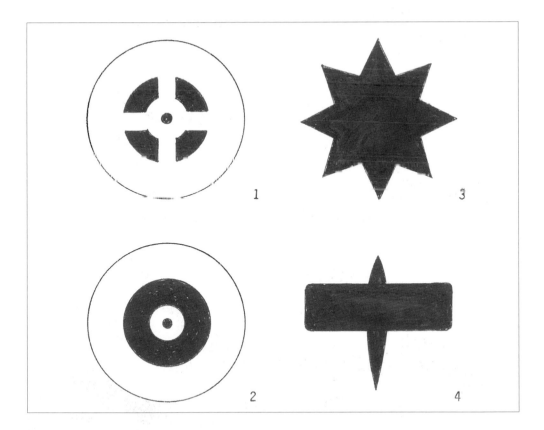

Operations Room plotting symbols. Although not positively identified these are believed to indicate 1. Aerodrome, 2. Landing field, 3. Bombs dropped, 4. Individual aeroplane. (Author's collection)

Clearly the *ad hoc* arrangements described above were not sufficient protection and, eventually, observation posts were established. It was not for some time, however, that the first of these came into use. From the few detailed records surviving, it is possible to state that the first post was established on 31 January 1916 at Croydon, Surrey, 14 miles distant from London proper. This was manned each night from 7 p.m. by a crew of Special Constables under the command of a 'specially trained officer', until midnight.

During previous potential attacks, Special Constables had kept watch, not only for aircraft, but also outbreaks of fire. They moved to high points which commanded an overall view of a district, and were provided with a telephone allowing direct contact with the Chief Inspector of the police, some areas even providing a car to take officers swiftly to any necessary site.

Thus the idea of a national defence network was slowly developing, but it was not until August 1917 that the first stage in creating a new defence system was complete. The London Air Defence Area (LADA) sought to centralise control of aircraft (three Flights each at Sutton's and Hainault Farms and on Hounslow Heath), guns, searchlights (in a belt stretching from Sussex to Northumberland, 25 miles inland from the coast), and the Metropolitan Observation Service, commanded by Lieutenant Commander Henry Paget, OBE, RNVR.

The latter organisation was to be staffed (three men to a post) entirely by Army personnel, and was to prove something of a disaster, partly due to the intake consisting of soldiers of a low medical standard, and also to being given only the most rudimentary instruction. Major General Ashmore, LADA's commander,[*] described them as 'of poor intelligence and worse discipline', and by December responsibility for the work at the 200 posts created by the new system had reverted largely to the regular police.

It is not difficult to explain why the service faced problems; not only did the spacing of posts make supervision problematic but, over and above the restrictions imposed by the medical condition of the men, the most fundamental handicap was their Army training, which, at that time, did not teach individuality in any form. Responsibility for the scheme fell to the police because all members of the force, including Special Constables, were trained to operate with individual responsibility, appraising a situation swiftly, and later rendering accurate reports. Ultimately, only a small number of posts retained military personnel, these men being drawn from two special companies, and ordered to work at posts where continuous watch was maintained, all others being manned only during an attack or when one was considered likely.

---

[*] Major General Edward Baily Ahsmore, the son of the Vicar of Tandridge, Surrey, entered the Royal Artillery in 1891, serving with 'Q' Battery of the RHA in South Africa, where he was severely wounded on 31 March 1900. On 3 September 1912, he obtained his pilot's certificate on Bristol Boxkite No.281, flying from Brooklands. 'Splash' Ashmore (the RA term for a direct hit) retired from the army in 1928 becoming a member of the LDVs (later Home Guard, May 1940) A fellow of the Philharmonic Society, he died at his home in Arundel, Sussex on 5 October 1953, aged eighty-one.

It is interesting to note what was required of observers, and intriguing that, at the time that these schemes were established, little technical detail was expected about the type of aircraft sighted. Reports of a 'plane' were sufficient, a procedure still followed in the very earliest days of the Second World War by the Observer Corps (not 'Royal' until 9 April 1941). Indeed, to possess a skill for accurate identification of specific types of aircraft was not so highly prized in the First World War as it was in later conflicts. The first posters designed to aid identification could only describe in general terms the aeroplanes and airships illustrated, while *The Aircraft Identification Book*, by Borlase Matthews and G. Clarkson, a pioneering identification guide, had to wait until 1919 for publication.

The LADA concept came about in a curious way, stemming from the time when King George V, visiting his troops in France, had been thrown from his horse during an inspection of No.2 Squadron at Hesdigneul, as recounted by an eyewitness named Butcher:

At the first roar, I noticed the almost imperceptible movement of the rear hooves of a frightened horse. Then, before any of us realised what was happening, the animal reared up, the immaculate picket rope flashing between the pawing front legs, before crashing to the ground on top of the King, and rolling over him. I was one of the NCOs who helped push the horse off and carry His Majesty to his car.

Apart from his own CO, Major J.H.W. Beck, Butcher had little idea of the identities of the officers in the party that rushed to the king's assistance, but we now know that one of these was Major Ashmore, and it was his subsequent witnessing of an unmarked Henry Farman innocently penetrating the protective barrier of air patrols and anti-aircraft artillery that was immediately thrown about the chateau at Aire where the king lay, which prompted him to write: 'It shows that aeroplane patrols are important in defence unless they are helped by an elaborate and far-reaching system of observation and control on the ground'.

Despite such shrewd deductions, based on thoughtful observation at first hand, his efforts to establish the LADA scheme were not unopposed. Crucial support, however, came from Lord John French, who had recently been ordered home from France to make way for Sir Douglas Haig, and who was now given responsibility for creating a new defence system, with the assistance of General Sir F. Shaw as his Chief of Staff.

As described earlier, the scheme relied heavily on the telephone system provided by the Electrical Engineering Department of the General Post Office, since it was necessary that reports of enemy aircraft sightings should be made to a central point. The location reports were ultimately directed to was the Operations Room in Spring Gardens, London, SW, which lay less than 100 yards from Admiralty Arch. Lieutenant Colonel M. St L. Simon, who had also been brought from France in January 1916, and was to become the system's artillery commander, left a description of the Operations Room, which had been based on a design by Major James:

On the south wall [was] a large map of the British Isles. On the east wall, a map capable of illumination, to illustrate the districts of Britain in accordance with their status; 'Under Warning' (green) and 'Under Orders' (red) which the C-on-C issued on reading the information on the large map.

In the centre of the room were chairs and tables for the officers conducting operations [while] just outside were telephone cabinets [where they] received reports... as they were switched through.

Thus: A report came in from the cabinets. The place names were hunted up in a Gazetteer for verification. The position of the airship (showing the time) was plotted on the large map. Pin 'A' went into this place on the map. Pin 'B' gave course [and] time of observation. Sequence of pins 'A' gave course and speed.

Reports from observation posts and 'reporters' (Army observers at each gun station, of which there were about forty-five, as well as at the 120 searchlight posts) went directly to an ancillary operations room supervised by a commander and sub-commander. Reports from these points were then telephoned to the Headquarters at Spring Gardens where they were received by an operator in the appropriate cabinet.

Each of these 'reporters' on duty at the observation posts was equipped with a small glass-topped and illuminated table, containing an ordnance map of the surrounding area, on which was superimposed a grid, while above was a height-finder to determine the altitude of aircraft. These devices replaced the multitudinous items of equipment, some home-made but nevertheless often efficient, with which civilian posts were originally equipped.

A perfected form of this system, first introduced by November 1916, became operational in late July the following year, resulting in a Headquarters Operations Room similar in layout and equipment to those of the 1920s and 1930s, although exact details are now lost. Surviving illustrations indicate that the areas into which plotting maps were divided were square and to a scale which dictated that the sides covered a distance of 4 miles. This was surrounded by ten plotters in telephone communication with the twenty-six sub-central Operations Rooms. The long-range board on the wall was to a scale of 2in to the mile.

In all likelihood therefore the LADA 'Air Bandit' control rooms were similar to Royal Observer Corps Operation Rooms between 1925 and 1965. RAF aerodromes were marked with special discs, while cruciform symbols indicated individual fighter aircraft. Plain discs were used to mark the tracks of enemy machines. Squares, formations of these, and five-point stars probably indicated targets under attack.

Oblong plaques were laid on the main table showing the actual routes of aircraft, these being employed according to the colour sequences given on a clock, where five-minute periods were shown as being either green, red or yellow, only two colours being simultaneously permitted on the table, so that 'stale' or 'faded' tracks did not remain to clutter the view.

On a raised dais overlooking this activity sat a police representative in direct communication with Divisional Headquarters and the Fire Brigade, beside General Ashmore and his deputy, Brigadier-General (later Air Commodore)

A wartime Special Constable who appears to be wearing a civilian overcoat and boots. He is accompanied by a Private of the Wiltshire Regiment. (Author's collection)

T.C.R. Higgins, who had been a qualified pilot even longer than his chief, having taken Royal Aero Club Certificate No.88 in a Farman biplane at Hendon on 16 May 1911. After June 1918, when the Biggin Hill transmitter began operating, he was in direct contact with interceptor stations by means of 'wireless telephones'.

Also on this platform sat recorders entering details of the tracks below them on miniature maps, with pencils appropriate to the colour phase shown on the master clock.

States of alert aided organisation, 'readiness' indicating that troops and the police were on standby, 'green' that an attack was threatened, 'red' that one was imminent, and 'white' that raiders were clear of the area. 'Yellow' cancelled 'green' to 'white' alerts, 'turn-in' doing the same for 'readiness'. The use of code-words in reports, for example 'daffodil' coming to represent 'sound of an aircraft', made the handling of information faster than ever before.

Ultimately, the evolved 'Air Bandit' system represented a bold and largely successful solution to a new problem, as well as now making it possible for the Home Office to give warnings of impending air attack to the general public. The Home Office were perhaps mindful of Winston Churchill's advice to the Commons on 30 June 1917: 'There ought to be a clear instruction from the Government as to what people are to do when an air raid takes place'.

Comprehensive public instruction had not been offered before, largely due to a fear among the authorities that such information would create large-scale panic,

A horse-drawn fire engine is manoeuvred into position. The men wear brass helmets and the pump is steam-powered. Horse-drawn appliances were being phased out during the First World War, but many still remained with the smaller brigades. (Author's collection)

it being regarded as almost better for people to be taken by surprise. Once again it fell to the police to give the necessary warning to the public in and around London.

From 21 July 1917, warning was to be given by firing a pair of maroons – the special loud rockets commonly used to summon lifeboat crews – with a gap of about five seconds between, from selected police stations. These firings were not at first sounded after 11 p.m., and indeed by September their use had tended to lapse, but they were resumed after 18 December, and by March the following year they began to be fired at any hour, but the manner in which they came into regular use is a curious one.

With effect from 25 September 1917, all fire brigades in the 750sq. mile area of London had been amalgamated under the Defence of the Realm Act, and it appears that responsibility for firing the maroons was either additionally or experimentally extended to the joint service, all stations of which were linked by telephone. This state of affairs perhaps indicates that it was not deemed practical to further burden the police at this time.

Although the end of September was given as the date of the official amalgamation of the fire brigades, on 22 July, having received a telephone warning from the Commissioner of Police, no less than seventy-nine fire stations duly gave warning of a raid with the aid of some 250 maroons. In fact an attack on London never materialised, nor was one intended. The source of the trouble was a German formation which crossed the coast of Suffolk at roughly 8 a.m., before turning south. Bombs were dropped on the beach at Felixstowe, on the town and on the naval air station, with thirty nine killed and injured here, as well as others at Harwich. It was all over in some ten minutes, and the twenty-one Gothas, having wrought £2,780 of damage, headed for home unscathed despite a number of interception sorties mounted by the defenders.

Responsibility for public warnings thereafter rested with the police, and did so for the remainder of the conflict. In built-up areas this was to be augmented during daylight, following an attack on 7 July 1917, by an 'emergency expedient', namely constables riding bicycles and wearing large placards bearing the words 'Police Notice. Take Cover', while blowing their whistles to attract attention. Cars were also used, carrying similar notices on their bonnets, often driven by the AA (Automobile Association) section of the Special Constabulary, which had been created by AA staff who had volunteered as Specials. That an attack was over was signalled by Boy Scouts, plus some members of the Church Lads' Brigade, who toured the streets, mostly on bicycles, sounding on their bugles the letters 'G-C' in Morse code (dash-dash-dot), followed by the three notes repeated, the letters having no alphabetical significance, being merely a set of easily identified notes. Simultaneously, locomotive whistles sounded a 'cock-a-doodle-do' and police went round again, this time displaying their 'all clear' placards.

The complete procedure was later copied in many other areas. Interestingly, the British use of bugles having been itself copied from the French (after trials with car horns had proved unsuccessful), following complaints that the notices could

Assembling a German 300kg (660lb) PuW (Pruefanstalt und Werft) high explosive bomb before loading into the racks of a Gotha. They had angled fins which are said to have improved aiming accuracy. (Author's collection)

not be read after dark, but outside Greater London's Metropolitan Police district, several novel ideas for audible warnings had been explored and trialled, including factory 'hooters' and sounding the sirens of ships on the Thames. Other suggestions were considered but not tested, such as switching on street lights during daylight, the use of gunfire, coloured smoke signals, or the raising of captive balloons as signals. The ringing of church bells was suggested as a warning to bank staff in the City that they should return money to the safes.

Beyond the metropolis, impending attack was signalled in some areas by constables on bicycles ringing hand-bells, while other districts saw a need for a 'first warning' to be given in advance of the 'take cover' notice, some reports referring to the use in some parts of the South East of 'horns' to indicate the likelihood of aerial attacks, possibly indicating some form of siren, such as was adopted in much-beleaguered Dover, where the factory 'hooter' of the electricity works gave four short blasts, followed by one long to give public warning of an expected attack.

Two police constables and a sergeant demonstrate firing maroons as a warning of an anticipated air raid at Croydon, Surrey. (Courtesy London Borough of Croydon)

Dover was the subject of an amusing tale in which an inhabitant, finding a small unexploded bomb and considering it his public duty to take it to his local police station, popped it into a sack and did just this. Here he flung it on the floor, to the distress of all concerned, so that there were suddenly very few to hear his repeated diagnosis of the situation. Happily the bomb turned out to be quite harmless due to a manufacturing fault, and the man's analysis of the situation was surprisingly correct!

The London system of using maroons to give warning of the approach of raiders had only been introduced the day before the multiple fire stations incident. Hitherto the policy had been to restrict any such alarms to fire and police services, railways, hospitals and arms factories. Despite the degree of near-panic that their use could and did create, the effectiveness of the system had soon been demonstrated, although it was clear that much of the public consternation was due to the number of rockets fired and the consequent noise they created.

It will have been made abundantly clear that among the little-remembered services that made up London's defences were the observation organisations in general and the Metropolitan Observer Service in particular. It is fortunate that a report of a night's work at one such post survives. This was one which, some 10 miles across country from central London, was sited at the top of the local town hall's 176ft clock tower. The date of the report is Whit Sunday, 19 May 1918, and the Special Constables on duty during the period were numbers 681, 1057, 1112, 1141, 1302 and 1596. The 'bearings' described were the numbers of the 16sq. mile grids superimposed on the maps of the surrounding areas.

The report covers three busy hours and is slightly edited here, contemporary spellings being retained. Notes in square brackets are the author's:

11.12 p.m.	Aeroplane on bearing 102 shewing lights – Bright lights on bearing 15 – Signal Rockets seen in South East [towards Sevenoaks, Kent].
11.23 p.m.	Gun flashes on bearing 102 very distant.
11.25 p.m.	Heavy gun fire on bearing 65 to 80 – Sounds of gun fire North East – Searchlights operating in the North East [perhaps Woolwich].
11.28 p.m.	Light on bearing 15 just extinguished. Continuous gun fire in the North East district.
11.29 p.m.	Sounds of distant gun fire in the North East district. On bearing 48 operating.
11.31 p.m.	Glow in bearing 15 very distant – Gun fire now to the North bearing 3 [Cental London] – Blaze on bearing 19 is now brighter – Gun flashes on bearing 3 to 5.
11.38 p.m.	Aeroplane on bearing 124 to 125 – Gun fire had been continuous on bearing 345 to 105.
11.40 p.m.	Local gun 3 miles distant to North North-West operating.
11.47 p.m.	Blaze reported on bearing 19 cannot now be seen.
11.48 p.m.	Two white signal lights on bearing 115 – Searchlight concentrating to the West – Local searchlight [just over 1 mile distant] operating – Flash on bearing 19 LOOKS MORE THAN A GUN FLASH – Gun fire getting much nearer but no shrapnel seen.
11.49 p.m.	Big glow, as if a bomb dropped on bearing 10 – Local A/A gun [less than 1 mile away to the North West] operating.
11.50 p.m.	Shrapnel bursting on altitude 45 [this probably means 45°, but could mean 4,500ft] – Searchlight on bearing 151 to 162.
11.51 p.m.	Signal lights on bearing 115.
11.52 p.m.	Both local guns in operation.
11.55 p.m.	Glow on bearing 9 – Shrapnel in the North East, altitude 45 – Another flash, as if a bomb had fallen on bearing 10 – Local A/A gun again in operation – Sounds of Aeroplane getting nearer from the North East; searchlights centering on them – Sound of big explosion in the North East – Tram-searchlight operating [it ran a half-mile route south from its depot which was

	1 mile south of the observers' post] – Aeroplane above referred to thought to be very near us. (20/5/18)
12.0 midn't	Signal-light on bearing 45 fairly near – Aeroplane mentioned above thought to be more distant.
12.03 a.m.	Very heavy gun fire in the North East and North West.
12.05 a.m.	Searchlight tram extinguished [probably due to a faulty mirror].
12.07 a.m.	Aircraft hum in the North West seems to be getting nearer again.
12.08 a.m.	Local gun operating again – Very heavy gun fire in the North East bearing 290.
12.10 a.m.	White signal light on bearing 30 – Gun flashes on bearing 138 very distant – Sounds of aircraft in the North – Sounds of aircraft getting closer in the North East.
12.13 a.m.	Searchlight tram in operation – Shrapnel bursting on altitude 50 the North East.
12.15 a.m.	Aeroplane travelling due East.
12.17 a.m.	Shrapnel bursting on bearing 64 altitude 30.
12.20 a.m.	Red signal light and white signal light on bearing 32 – On bearing 32 thought to be an aeroplane BROUGHT DOWN ON FIRE – White signal light on bearing 115 – Very heavy gun fire in the North East but too distant to see the flashes – Gun flashes from the North East to North – Sounds of aircraft in the North East – Gun firing extending to the North West on bearing 345.
12.25 a.m.	Signal light on bearing 50 On bearing 27 a flash seen; looked very much like an explosion – Both local guns in operation.
12.27 a.m.	On bearing 97 lights in the sky, looks as if it was one of our aeroplanes.
12.30 a.m.	Half a dozen white rockets on bearing 95 – Sounds of aircraft in the North and North East coming this way.
12.34 a.m.	Shrapnel bursting in the North, altitude 27.
12.35 a.m.	Another glow on bearing 10, very distant, looked like a bomb having been dropped.
12.36 a.m.	Sounds of aircraft dying away – Sounds of aircraft in the East getting nearer.
12.39 a.m.	Both local guns in operation – Shrapnel bursting in the North East, altitude 45.
12.48 a.m.	Gun flashes very distant, North and North West of London.
12.55 a.m.	Signal light on bearing 110 high up – Gun fire very distant North and North East – Signal light or Rocket on bearing 115.
12.58 a.m.	All quiet, but distant searchlights, North, North East.
1.00 a.m.	Light on aircraft on bearing 105 – Two very distant flickering lights on bearing 53 on the horizon – Sounds of aircraft in the South East, thought to be one of our own.
1.10 a.m.	One of our aeroplanes travelling East shewing a light – Two signal lights on bearing 94.
1.19 a.m.	ALL CLEAR.

1.32 a.m.	Order to SOUND MAROONS. ON DUTY AGAIN – All crew returned to their respective places.
1.38 a.m.	Gun flashes and searchlights in the South East – Red and white signal lights in the North East – Gun flashes on bearing 165 – Gun fire due South.
1.41 a.m.	Shrapnel bursting South East bearing 165, altitude 16 – Sounds of aircraft in the South – Local searchlight operating – Searchlight tram operating – Sounds of aircraft South East, almost East – Sounds of aircraft disappearing North East.
1.45 a.m.	All searchlights extinguished – Bright light reported in local street on bearing 3, about 150 yards away.
1.50 a.m.	Distant searchlight operating between [bearings] 40 and 80.
1.55 a.m.	Gun flash on bearing 135.
1.58 a.m.	Local searchlight in operation and several others in the North – White signal light on bearing 31 – light on bearing 3 is now extinguished.
1.58 a.m.	Searchlights are now signalling.
2.00 a.m.	ALL CLEAR.
2.09 a.m.	DISMISS.

Signed: H.E.T. Wilcox (1596).

Unknowingly, these men were witnesses to a piece of history: this was the last attack on England's capital for twenty-two years. The note in the log at 12.20 a.m. – 'looked like an aeroplane brought down on fire' was certainly accurate; what they were watching was the end of a Gotha brought down by a Bristol F.2B C4636 of No.39 Squadron crewed by Lieutenant A.J. Arkell and 1st Air Mechanic A.T.C. Stagg. The enemy aircraft had crashed at exactly the time Wilcox had recorded, falling in a cabbage field beside Roman Way, East Ham, the rear fuselage breaking off as it did so. This fell some 50 yards distant from the main heap, which formed a carbonated pile covering an area of some 12sq. yards.

One engine had also fallen free and lay some distance off, becoming a feature of intense interest for the hundreds who flocked to see the area on the Whit Monday after the raid, the actual location of the wreckage being uselessly described in the next day's morning papers as 'an open space not many miles from London', although its whereabouts were by then well-known.

Of the crew, whose demise was recorded with glee in the same papers, only one of the gunners, Gefreiter Wilhelm Schulte, was to die in the crash, Leutnant Paul Sapkowiak and Vizfeldwebel Hans Thiedke jumping to their deaths before the impact, the preceding minutes of which were recorded in a morning newspaper the next day thus, headed 'Raiders Fall In Flames' and 'Graphic Stories of Thrilling Battles in the Air':

Of the four Gothas destroyed that Sunday night one was brought to earth within full view of a district, and its fall called forth a great burst of cheering.

A vivid story is told of the cornering of this raider. Its 'downing' was most dramatic, and provided a fitting culmination to some effective gunnery from below and wonderful manoeuvring of our flying men above.

One side of London a perfect crescendo of guns firing left no doubt in the minds of the watchers that the enemy had been driven into a corner. Suddenly the searchlights flashed out to play their part in the affair, and then it could be seen that there was a formation of Gothas flying at a comparatively low altitude with a number of British machines above. Our own men appeared to be sitting on their opponents, awaiting the opportunity to administer the death-blow. They had not long to wait.

This highly colourful but uninformative style of writing attempted to satisfy public thirst, and in fact dealt with an encounter between just two aircraft, which had begun with Arkell noting the exhausts of a raider below him at 10,000ft. Diving down, Stagg had the opportunity to fire off half a drum under the tail of the raider, before the British pilot turned away and attacked with the Bristol's front gun. Arkell managed to put in a number of bursts with this, despite return fire from the Gotha's two defensive positions, before turning in order to allow Stagg to loose off several complete drums under the raider's tail.

The encounter had now dropped to only 1,500ft when one of the Gotha's engines was seen to be ablaze and the aircraft went into a series of flat spins before crashing – one of the total of seven claimed to have been accounted for that night (three, it was alleged, into the sea) for a cost of thirty-seven killed and 155 injured. These were the casualty figures reported at the time, but modern research indicates figures of forty-nine killed and 177 injured.

These night sorties by Bogohl 3 were intended, as British Intelligence was to state at the time, to be a maximum effort, for which thirty-eight Gothas were despatched on the night in question in company with three Staaken Giants, one with a 1,000kg (2,200lb) bomb aboard. In fact, only twenty-eight Gothas actually crossed the coast, and although the force of three Giants remained intact, only one is said to have reached London, the remaining pair attacking targets in Essex and Kent, Chelmsford believed to have received the 2,000 pounder.

Subsequent British reports are surprisingly accurate, claiming that 'about 30 raiders' made up the attacking force, although the official claim of 'considerable damage to house property' is at odds with the dismissive attitude of the press, with papers stating that the raiders over Kent dropped bombs at various places 'without material damage', while those that had penetrated to London had scattered 'a few dozen bombs promiscuously'. However, the temptation to shock readers was to prove too much for some, one newspaper recalling how 'in one district seven people were killed by bombs which demolished two houses [and] from the debris the police recovered six bodies, [while] next door the body of a woman was taken out… In an adjoining street another bomb did damage to property, and four persons were removed to hospital'.

However, by this point of the First World War, the freedom to give details of the locations of such incidents was withdrawn, and these could now only be hinted at. Thus we learn that 'a Metropolitan hospital suffered as the result of one of the bombs.

NOTHING is to be written on this side except the date and signature of the sender. Sentences not required may be erased. If anything else is added the post card will be destroyed.

I am quite well.

I have been admitted into hospital
{ ~~sick~~ } *and am going on well.*
{ *wounded* } ~~and hope to be discharged soon.~~

I am being sent down to the base.

I have received your { *letter dated* 4/5/15
{ *telegram ,,* _____
{ ~~parcel~~ *,,* _____

X *Letter follows at first opportunity.* X

~~I have received no letter from you~~
{ ~~lately.~~
{ *for a long time.*

Signature }
only. }   *Will*

Date _____ 9th May 1915

[Postage must be prepaid on any letter or post card addressed to the sender of this card.]

(25343) Wt. W3497–293 1,760m. 4/15 M.R.Co.,Ltd.

Buff-coloured postcards such as this were the first intimation received at home that a member of the family had been wounded. (Author's collection)

A large number of windows were smashed by the concussion, and patients and staff were much alarmed, but fortunately no serious personal casualties were reported'.

Thus ended the final aeroplane attack of the First World War, the last assault by airships being delayed until the beginning of August, when the Midlands were the target. Soon after the May assault, the British crews were to receive suitable decorations from the fifty-three-year-old King George V. The incident which took place twenty minutes after midnight on 20 May has been described above, and, for this, pilot Tony Arkell received the Military Cross, and his gunner Stagg, the Military Medal.

Twenty-five minutes later, Lieutenant Eric Turner of No.141 Squadron, at the controls of Bristol F.2B C851, with observer Barwise, were to see the end of Gotha GV 979/16, which crashed near Frinsted, some 8 miles east of Maidstone. This had been entirely due to accurate shooting from Barwise with his Lewis gun, which jammed after three bursts of fire. For this action, the pair were subsequently awarded the Distnguished Flying Cross, a decoration which had only been instituted on 3 June 1918.

Examination of the partially burnt remains of this Gotha, at first posed a problem for those responsible, since it was prominently marked 'FST' until it was realised that this was no service identification but a combination of the initials of the crew; Leutnant Joachim Flathow, observer, Vizefeldwebel Albrecht Sachtler, the pilot, and Unteroffizier Hermann Tasche, the gunner and only member of the trio to escape with his life. Reports stated that this raider had been briefly intercepted by an SE5a of No.143 Squadron.

Admiralty Arch where part of the Home Defence administrative control were accommodated in bleak offices. (Author's collection)

A Zeppelin in flight as portrayed by Hans Rudolf Schuze, a specialist of the period dealing with aviation and natural history subjects. (Author's collection)

Sheds and a Sopwith Baby floatplane wrecked by a pair of 12kg bombs dropped on Felixstowe RNAS Station on 4 July 1917. A flying boat was destroyed at its moorings while six ratings and three civilian workmen were killed in the same attack. (Bruce Robertson collection)

The third award for the night's work was that of the Distinguished Service Order to Major C.J.O. Brand who, flying a standard Sopwith F.1 Camel (that is to say not a version specially adapted for night-flying) numbered D6423, encountered a Gotha seven minutes before midnight on 19 May when he opened fire, setting the enemy alight three minutes later to crash near to the Harty Landing Ground, named after the nearby village of the same name on the Isle of Sheppey.

However, there was another of the raiders which prematurely fell on that night. This was Gotha GV 925/16 which crashed at St Osyth, not due to any action by the defenders but as a result of a navigational error. Lost in cloud, the crew of the *Pommern*,[*] Leutnant Wilhelm Rist, the pilot, and his two companion Vizefeldwebels, Max Gummelt and Rudolf Huhnsdorfs, lost altitude attempting to determine their whereabouts. It was while doing this that the unfortunate Rist made a mistake that was to cost him his life, accidentally choking the starboard motor, and despite jettisoning the load, he failed to gain altitude, and the aircraft crashed at ten minutes before midnight on 19 May.

Anti-aircraft defences played a notable part in repelling the raiders, with batteries claiming that their victims had crashed into the sea off Dover, Shoeburyness and Foreness Point, Kent. The latter is a minor promontory some 2 miles east of Margate lighthouse. This particular crash is not confirmed by German records.

This historic night's work would serve as an example of effective national defence, and the lessons learned would be crucial not only to those studying the night-interception techniques of the six-week-old Royal Air Force, but also to those organising the Army's searchlight units and the new audio-interception procedures.

---

[*] An identification of the significance of this name is that the crew were natives of that part of Prussia which lay south of the Baltic coast and north of Brandenburg which is known thus. This is anglicised as 'Pomerania'.

FIVE

SHELTERS AND SHELTERERS

By 1917 civilians had still not yet begun to realise that attacks on Britain henceforth had to be accepted as part of 'total warfare', and there was a general perception that more could be done to prevent attacks completely. This public sentiment was expressed when a hostile crowd descended on an anti-aircraft position in Hyde Park demanding that the gunners open fire on a friendly aircraft overhead, this with such vehemence that the men felt their lives were in danger. None of this mass hysteria was reflected in the tone adopted by the newspapers, although these had ceased to report air attacks with the shocked bewilderment that had characterised earlier articles.

The apparent change of outlook in the press was perhaps the result of a realisation that the defences were capable of hitting back, and that casualty figures could be reduced by the provision of adequate shelters. Readers were left in no doubt, however, that the press as a whole believed the authorities were lax in formulating defence measures. The severest criticism of government policy related to the lack of provision of shelter during bombing raids. The announcement that a Wight seaplane and a Bristol TB8 (number 1224) had been allocated for air defence following a bold attempt to bomb the Admiralty Pier at Dover using a Friedrichshafen FF29 from Scaplane Unit No.1 during daylight on 21 December 1914, triggered public discontent. The outcry grew in volume as time passed, and as the population endured nocturnal visits by airships, which were later replaced by Gotha aeroplanes in the first major raid on London on 13 June three years later, a daylight attack which resulted in seventeen raiders successfully penetrating the defences to drop 6,600 tons of high explosive on the capital, resulting in the deaths of 162 civilians and 432 injured.

The attacks eventually prompted the construction of private refuges where groups of people gathered, these approximating to the public street shelters of the Second World War. The provision by the government of individual family shelters was limited solely to the later conflict. Of the communal retreats several descriptions survive. A typical example of a shelter, this one set up in north London adjacent to a school, the grounds of which were bordered on one side by a main railway line, is described below:

> Two railway arches are in our playground, so we set to work, and in about ten days we had a 9ft wall about 4ft thick in front of each [arch] and a similar screen in front of an entrance at the back. It took about 1,600 sandbags, and if we had bought all the bags and sand it would have cost us £130. We bought the sacking and made the bags. The Borough Surveyor gave us breeze (cinders) from the rubbish incinerator, which is much better than sand and the bags were filled at the refuse collection site. As far as they could, the staff helped cart the filled bags to our place, but they could not do it fast enough and a firm in the parish came to our rescue and carted the remaining lot free of charge.
>
> The boys of the school, the schoolmaster and I or any man or lad carried the filled bags in, work that had to be done in the day, and in addition to some of the older boys, the police came to our aid between the hours of duty, their height and strength proving especially useful in heaving the heavy bags up when required. On one occasion we were on the job for five hours without interruption – and that was the second shift of the day! On Saturday afternoons, sidesmen, the Boys' Brigade lads and club members all came and worked with a will, while the women workers who had cut the bags and made them up were on hand to sew the faulty ones.
>
> Another firm gave us three hundred old sacks while [yet] other firms gave us money, so that when I at last came to pay the bill which was for £27, one of the partners said 'We ought not to make a profit out of this, so we'll take £20 and give you a credit note for £7', with the result that our £130 fortifications came to about £24!
>
> The work put new life into the parish, the people instead of getting worried and anxious had been distracted by it all and finally to celebrate the completions of our efforts, we gave a 'dug-out' dance!
>
> We can accommodate five hundred people comfortably in our two railway arch dug-outs which are warmed with braziers and have access under cover to a kitchen and other conveniences.

But not all areas were as well-placed as this in having buildings capable of modification, other districts resorting to cleaning-out, warming and making habitable the basements of churches, one account running:

> We have had the dingy walls of the crypt cleaned and whitewashed, we have introduced electric light to illuminate the subterranean darkness, and the people have continued the transformation by cleaning out the rubbish, removing the great ventilation boxes (an idea of years ago) re-arranged the layout and fitted up a most comfortable kitchen.

Similar adaptations to provide shelter were made to some church halls or rectories, the majority of the latter being of sturdy construction. The vicar of a parish to the north of that mentioned above wrote:

Mail carts such as this were used to take such a quantity of personal items to the Underground railway shelters that they eventually had to be banned. (Author)

I took the opportunity of consulting a firm of experts engaged in a large amount of air-raid protection work. They arranged to sandbag the sub-basement windows of the rectory, and do other protection work about the church, which is very strongly built and affords good cover. Since these arrangements have been made, the rectory basement has always been open for people, numbering 100, under the direction of my wife.

We only allow women with babies and young children into the stoke-hole, for that is the safest place, while even the porch above is filled and not long ago we took cover like this for ten nights in succession, lasting from four to six hours each night.

Another clergyman in a nearby parish recalled: 'In a large basement, cellar, and three huge rooms on the ground floor, on the staircases and in the passages, we are packed like sardines, sometimes for two hours, sometimes six, some 800 to 1,000 people'.

Provision for safe accommodation in churches during air raids placed a notable strain on the vicars of poorer parishes. The vicar of St Peter's, north-east London, states: 'It is by no means an easy thing to jump out of bed, throw on a dressing gown, rush down and open the doors, and stay in that crowded atmosphere [the crypt] for several hours'.

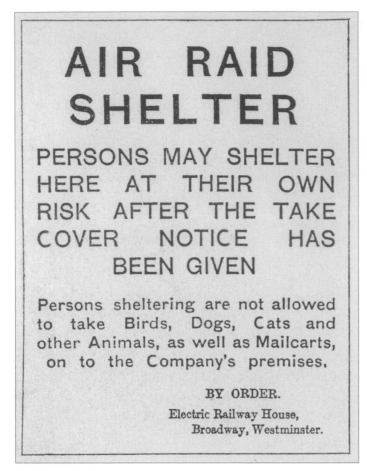

AIR RAID SHELTER

PERSONS MAY SHELTER HERE AT THEIR OWN RISK AFTER THE TAKE COVER NOTICE HAS BEEN GIVEN

Persons sheltering are not allowed to take Birds, Dogs, Cats and other Animals, as well as Mailcarts, on to the Company's premises.

BY ORDER.
Electric Railway House,
Broadway, Westminster.

Shelterers on railway premises were increasingly met with notices such as this at the station entrances. (Author's collection)

Other districts were extremely thorough, anticipating official measures and even laying the foundations of the Air-Raid Precautions of the conflict twenty years hence. This foresight resulted in the appointment of Marshals to control the crowds in North London. These same men had earlier been responsible for giving up their Saturday afternoons to dig a sloping path to give access to the crypt which otherwise had to be entered via a dangerous and cramped staircase. This ramp was completed with sandbags to protect vulnerable parts, with the path leading to the entrance being illuminated by the best subdued lighting that regulations allowed. It seems that exercises were organised to test the time taken to usher the public into the shelter; the shelter could accommodate 1,700 people comfortably in seventeen minutes, the record being 1,900 blind, crippled, aged or otherwise handicapped in the same space of time. The watchful eyes of the Marshals ensured good behaviour among the people, who proved 'content to await their turn and exercise self-control'. In the event of a reported pending attack, stewardesses who had been appointed at the same time as the Marshals also reported for duty to assist mothers and children. The volunteer force worked pre-determined periods of duty. A similarly well-organised shelter was described as 'the best 'ole in the neighbourhood'.

This entrance of a public air-raid shelter in Trinity Square, Margate, Kent, is properly equipped for the safety of users, including a hand rail at the side of the entrance slope. (Author's collection)

Better-known than the facilities provided by parish churches are the shelter arrangements made available in substantial private and public buildings by courtesy of their owners. Some of these were quite modest in size, being no more than the cellars of buildings erected in the previous century when these were commonplace, so that it was not unusual to find notices such as this posted at their entrance: 'This house contains a fairly good sized cellar. In the event of an air raid, passers-by are welcome to what shelter it affords'. Another, in 1915, ran: 'Air raids. During an air raid persons may take shelter in this Building at their own risk'. In contrast were the vast man-made caverns beneath Harrods in Knightsbridge.

Sanctuary outside the domestic field would frequently have its accommodation limits exhibited outside. These seem to have been surprisingly modest, perhaps reflecting an awareness of the dangers of overcrowding. The authorities initially had no knowledge of the internal dimensions of these locations so, in early July 1918, an inspection of many of these was undertaken, a note from the Metropolitan Police Commissioner's office commenting: 'It is evident that the numbers appearing on the posters must be meant to be the maximum safe numbers that can be accommodated in each shelter. It would be quite useless to post up any other figure. There is no doubt that all the shelters will hold more than the numbers scheduled'. Below is a list of seventeen private shelters in various types of private building distributed over five police Divisions, quoting their listed accommodation and the actual number sheltering at the time of the most recent attack. This had been the night attack of 19/20 May 1918 when twenty-eight of the thirty-eight Gothas despatched had raided London, killing forty-nine and wounding 177:

ACCOMMODATION OF VARIOUS SHELTERS

	Listed	Actual
166 Old Street, EC1	1,000	2,500
Wenlock Brewery, Wenlock Street, N1	1,500	3,500
Reeves Factory, Dalston, E8	150	1,000
Seaman Hospital	250	900
Gaymer and Co., Cambridge Heath Road, E1	600	3,000
St. Saviors Priory, Great Cambridge Street, N1	200	450
Bethnal Green Junction, Three Colts Lane, E2	150	700
Rowton House, Newington Causeway, SE1	1,000	4,000
Moffat Institute, Esher Street	150	500
Kempton Glass Warehouse, Dolland Street, SE1	350	1,500
Mumford's Mill, Albert Embarkment, SE1	200	600
Pembroke College Mission Hall, SE17	200	750
St. John's Institute, SE17	300	850
Bermondsey Town Hall, Spa Road, SE16	500	1,500
Chanton & Co., Dockley Road, SE16	200	900
Lecture Hall, Albert Road, SE8	100	300
Weslyan Church, Brockley Road, SE8	100	350

(Numbering of Postal Districts had begun in March 1917. It was officially explained that this was 'due to the use of temporary staff'.)

It seems likely that priority was given to the east and north of London, perhaps due to the proximity of the docks, which could be regarded as a legitimate military target, with the result that some of the inhabitants of these districts would make a nightly journey west. They would set off early if the moon was full and bright, the kind historically described as a 'hunter's moon' but now becoming known as a 'bomber's moon'.

Like the good airman and tactician he was, Hauptmann Rudolf Kleine, commander of Kagohl (Battle Squadron) No.3 had selected one such night of a full moon – 29/30 October 1917 – for the first in a series of massive attacks on England's capital. However, the attack was cancelled following an adverse weather forecast, so that only a nuisance raid by three aircraft was launched, and another unit made a light assault on Dover the following night.

The night attack of 31 October/1 November was much more determined and, in an attempt to reap some benefit from the moon, twenty-two Gothas were launched against London, about half of them carrying incendiaries, their approach route being via Dover, thus avoiding the main defence concentrations. Even so, the strong winds encountered blew that formation off course. This could perhaps account for the fact that, according to German reports, only half of their number found the target. As a result, the unfortunate East End was to suffer once again.

The bomb loads were made up of both incendiaries and high explosive, and a story survives of one example of the latter exploding in the middle of a street, only 4 yards from the door of a house where nine people were asleep in bed. The resultant explosion destroyed the entire front of the dwelling but, despite this, none were hurt, and it was a tale that was told and re-told the following morning, and officially emphasised in order to keep up public morale. Less lucky were the inhabitants of what was described in contemporary records as an 'especially dangerous spot'. Six children and an adult male were killed when a large bomb fell in the garden of a nearby rectory, although the three incendiaries which accompanied the high explosive caused no major fires, merely burning out in the roadway.

Word was spreading of a rising death toll (1,414 killed and 3,416 injured, according to post-war writers), so a substantial number of London's citizens began to make nightly trips to the underground railway system, most having decided that these tunnels would afford the greatest hope of protection during a bombing raid. Public interest in the underground railway during the First World War had initially been stimulated by reports of police searches in the tunnels, especially the disused sections of the City & South London Railway between King William Street and Borough, as early as the first week of August 1914, prompted by fears that they had been utilised by enemy agents for the storage of explosives or armour. Nothing was found, and two years later the C & SLR was to use some of the tunnels for the storage of rolling stock.

Shelter in the Tube

From the earliest air attacks on London, first by airships and then by aeroplanes, it had been the custom for stations of the underground railway system to offer shelter to people caught in the streets during a raid but, by September 1917, after five concentrated night attacks that seemed to herald an newly intensified campaign, the underground stations became a nightly home for whole families, who settled there whether or not an air raid warning had been given, and brought with them birds, dogs, cats, and other pets, together with small children in 'mailcarts'. In addition, bedding and individual life-savings were brought along, some bringing a supply of food, though usually only enough for one meal, as the attacks were of relatively short duration compared with the all-night raids of just over twenty years later.

Rather than become bored merely waiting on platforms, some whiled away their time by boarding trains, particularly on the Inner Circle Line (later absorbed into the Circle and District Lines), making unlimited circuits of the system, indulging en route in the refreshment they carried. Whether or not this is how they chose to spend the night, approximately 100,000 people are believed to have gone to ground in the London Tube system during the night attack of 24 September 1917, and 120,000 on the following night.

The situation was becoming grave with so many people crammed into the stations with no sanitation available and no provision for food, except that which they themselves had brought. The C & SLR stations in particular were 'not ventilated with fans, the masses blocking the platforms and stairways and interfering with the proper running of the trains'. Indeed, this misuse of the Underground system rapidly became part of the way of life for many families in the East End; children would make a habit of obtaining free rides back to their starting point, passing the time until the threat of an, often imagined, attack was judged to be over. For amusement en route, they would dodge from car to car at each stop playing 'last in' through the doors in the days when every carriage had its own guard who operated these manually by means of a large lever.

Quite apart from the tunnels under the river Thames, which were also used as shelters, an estimated number of 300,000 persons were regularly sheltering in the system as the autumn of 1917 arrived, choking the stations and making it impossible for travellers to reach, or alight from, those trains which continued to run.

One recollection of these circular journeys made by children has survived in the memoirs of Harry Errington (later to be awarded the George Cross for bravery shown as a fireman in the Blitz of the Second World War). This is recorded by Martin Lloyd-Elliott in his book *City Ablaze*, in which Harry recalls:

> We would dash as fast as we could to Oxford Circus Underground Station and down on to the platforms. It was so exciting as we could go on joy rides all along the line and back to pass the time until the raid was over.
>
> When we eventually returned to Oxford Circus, we would emerge into the streets and run around in great screaming gangs, collecting bits of shrapnel off the pavements and from the gutters, bantering all while as to whose was the hottest piece. It was always way past our bed-times and that.

This was not all, since large numbers of people had adopted the habit of regularly leaving the capital at night-fall and camping on the periphery, then still semi-rural in parts, crowding the trains back to London in the early morning and competing with regular travellers attempting to get to work.

Clearly firm measures had to be taken at once and, on 25 September, a start was made, with posters put up at Underground stations stating:

Air raid shelter. Persons may shelter here at their own risk after the take cover notice has been given', adding that 'Persons sheltering are not allowed to take Birds, Dogs, Cats and other animals, as well as Mailcarts, on to the Company's premises.

By Order,
Electric Railway House,
Broadway, Westminster.

Whatever the immediate results of these measures, the first steps at regularisation of the practice had already been taken on 3 November when the Commissioner of the Metropolitan Police declared that arrangements for this had already been made, a reference to the opening of negotiations with the underground railway companies on 25 October.

The new arrangements included the payment by the Home Office of £130 per week to reimburse the railway company for the cost of staffing and lighting the stations. This was agreed on 13 November when, at each of the eighty-one (recently eighty-six) stations involved, 'sufficient staff' was acknowledged to mean one railway employee and two police officers, who would be instructed that 'when 'Take Air Raid Action' had been ordered', they were 'not to tell the public that a warning had been officially issued'. This was clearly a precaution against panic, and the kind of behaviour described by a St John's Ambulance Brigade officer at the time: 'Everyone runs at once ... People arrive in a state of excitement which changes to hysteria when the guns begin to fire'.

It was about this time that a lady described as a Russian Jewess was reported to have been killed in a crush at one station. A few nights earlier, or so ran a tale which went the rounds, there had been several deaths in a rush for cover triggered, tragically, not by bombs but by the explosion of warning maroons.

Two posters measuring some 24in by 36in were quickly produced for display at the entrances to underground stations, one printed in black on white, stating: 'Air Raids. The Company will not be responsible for any accident, injury, or loss to persons or property', before going on to announce that shelterers must 'Obey, promptly, instructions given by the staff... Don't rush or push... Don't press against lift gates... Keep back from the edge of the platform... Keep gangways and stairways clear... Don't attempt to enter tunnels or go near live rails'. Of similar size, the second poster was intended for use at shallow Underground stations. It was red with white lettering, reading: 'Air raids. Owing to insufficient cover this station is unsuitable for the protection of persons sheltering during an air raid'.

By the beginning of 1917 it had become obvious that clarification was required regarding the several types of shelter available. An inspection programme resulted in the issuing of the following list of cover available at Underground railway stations, which set out the capacities of these shelters. It gives some idea of the number of Londoners making use of the system. It is headed 'Tube Stations Used as Air Raid Shelters in the Metropolitan Police Area', and goes on to give the capacity of each. Those marked 'CP' were administered by the City of London Police and would be the subject of a separate survey. Names of Underground Railway Lines are those in use at the time:

District Railway

Aldgate East	5,000
St Mary's	2,000
Stepney Green	500
Mile End	3,000
Bow Road	2,000

Bakerloo Line

Elephant & Castle	3,000*	Baker Street	2,500
Lambeth North	4,000	Marylebone	3,000
Waterloo	4,000	Edgware Road	3,000
Charing Cross	2,500	Paddington	2,000
Trafalgar Square	3,000	Maida Vale	1,000
Piccadilly Circus	5,000*	Warwick Avenue	2,000
Oxford Circus	3,000	Kilburn Park	500
Regents Park	1,000		

Piccadilly Line

Earl's Court	2,000	Covent Garden	2,000
Gloucester Road	3,000	Holborn	2,500
South Kensington	2,000	Aldwych	2,000
Brompton Road	2,000	Russell Square	3,000
Knightsbridge	2,000	King's Cross	9,000*
Hyde Park Corner	500	York Road	2,000
Down Street	1,000		
[closed 1932]		Holloway Road	2,000
Dover Street	1,000	Leicester Square	3,000
[renamed			
Green Park, 1933]			
Gillispie Road	4,000	Finsbury Park	12,000

[To these, Essex Road and Highbury were added later.]

---

*Total capacity of interchange station.

Hampstead Line

Charing Cross	2,500	Kentish Town South	4,000
Strand	2,000	Kentish Town	4,000
Tottenham Court Rd	3,000	Tufnell Park	4,000
Goodge Street	3,000	Highgate	4,000
Warren Street	4,000	Chalk Farm	1,000
Euston	3,000*	Belsize Park	1,750
Mornington Crescent	2,000	Hampstead	3,000
Camden Town	8,000		

Central London Railway

Liverpool Street	(CP)	Bond Street	2,000
Post Office	(CP)	Marble Arch	3,000
Chancery Lane	2,000	Lancaster Gate	2,000
British Museum	2,000	Queen's Road	2,000
Tottenham Court Rd	2,000		
Notting Hill Gate	2,000		
Oxford Circus	3,000	Holland Park	2,000
Shepherds Bush	3,000		

City & South London Railway

Angel	4,000	Kennington	2,000
City Road	4,000	Oval	1,750
Old Street	4,000	Stockwell	1,200
Moorgate Street	(CP)	Clapham Road	1,200
Bank	(CP)	Clapham Common	3,000
London Bridge	(CP)	Borough	1,500

There is little question that it was the weight of public opinion, not to say militancy in the East End, that had secured the Underground system for sanctuary during the aerial attacks on London. The authorities, seeing that they were faced with a *fait accompli*, had no alternative but to graciously accept defeat. There remained the problem of overcrowding, however, and, in an attempt at finding a solution, the authorities carried out a survey in the closing days of September 1917. Its findings gave an indication of the conditions which shelterers were prepared to tolerate, and also an idea of public perceptions regarding an enemy's ability to threaten their homes.

---

*Total capacity of interchange station.

On 28 September 1917, a visit to the C & SLR station at the Elephant & Castle, even at 6.25 p.m.[*] found it so packed that entry was difficult. There was little or no attempt being made to regulate the crowds and leave space for rail passengers, and a police officer from 'M' Division was sent to instruct the four Special Constables at the station in their duty, since they were seemingly inexperienced and had little idea of crowd control. Half an hour later, three regular PCs at Borough Station were found to be faced with a similar situation but, despite being under intense pressure due to the numbers involved, were slowly managing to introduce some order among the largely female crowd, a crowd described as being 'in a very excited state and leading their children'. Many had brought push-carts and supplies of food. Some time elapsed before the crowd could be convinced that the reigning confusion was dangerous. The bulk of their men-folk were away, the small number present being on their way to night work, 'so that', the report explained, 'consequently their wives were liable to give way to agitation'.

It was a little after 7 p.m. when the inspectors arrived at London Bridge Station, outside which people were calmly waiting in a queue for admittance under the direction of six Specials. Inside, however, the situation was more disorganised, with the station master finding it necessary to turn off the water at the main due to shelterers constantly leaving the platform water taps running, with the consequent danger of flooding. He found it very difficult to make the crowds understand the necessity for order, attributing this to the fact that the people who came each night were severely under-privileged and had never been accustomed to much order or discipline.

Half an hour later at Old Street the situation was quite different. Here, although the platforms and approaches were 'very full', the crowds were well controlled and orderly, leaving room for passengers to join or disembark from trains. At about 8.30 p.m. a similar situation was found at Finsbury Park, a state of affairs believed to be due to the presence of more family men. Similar situations prevailed at Highbury and Essex Road, although at the latter a substantial number of foreign men were present who proved to be resented by some of the crowd.

As a result of these reports it was advised that in future police should be on duty at the entrance to Underground stations by 5 p.m., when the crowds began to assemble. It was agreed that officers arriving later than this may find it difficult to keep order.

---

[*] Incidentally, the hours quoted are Greenwich Mean Time, Britain's second summer of daylight-saving (introduced for that year on 8 April) having ceased eleven days earlier. William Willett had conceived the idea of daylight saving in 1907, the same year that the first Bill proposing its introduction was tabled in the Commons. This, like those of 1910 and 1911, was defeated, only King Edward VII using the system privately in Royal Households. The wartime adoption of 'Mad Willett's' plan, fourteen years after his death and only some twenty-five years after that of Greenwich Mean Time, lasted until 1925 and was initially unpopular as 'Prussian Time'. Strangely, Willett is recorded as having written before 1914 that the longer days resulting from his proposed time change would give more time for rifle practice for which 'the nation may one day have case to be thankful'.

The shortage of sanitation was also considered, the assembly of such large numbers of people without adequate facilities of this kind creating a situation which the report describes as 'very unpleasant'. In addition, the provision of first aid was examined, following a large number of cases of fainting, and it was argued that one or two members of St John's Ambulance or the Red Cross could be usefully employed. That services such as these were necessary is indicated by the writer who, some twenty years later, recalled the capital's Underground railway system as having been 'ill-lit with filthy carriages and platforms, the trains proceeding at a crawling pace, in an atmosphere more heavily charged with poisonous fumes than even the very worst 'London particulars' [fogs] outside'. A more detached view of the shelters comes from J.M. Grider, an American pilot serving with No.85 Squadron RAF. Written in late summer 1918, a passage in his *Diary of an Unknown Aviator* describes how, as the warning maroons were fired at about 10.30 p.m., the girls he and some friends were visiting 'jumped like they had been hit already', and grabbed some camp stools, saying they were going down in the tube station. The men said that they were not going, but the girls begged them to do so. Eventually the men agreed to take cover and 'took along a bottle of whisky and a plate of cake, the girls hysterical with fright'. The station 'was already packed', and they were unable to get down to the platform, so the party 'camped on a landing half-way down'. Here the air proved so foul after a time that they all decided to leave. Grider describes the city above ground: 'Outside, the town was absolutely deserted. We waited fifteen minutes for a taxi but there wasn't any so we had to walk home… the city was like a sepulchre except for the terrible racket of the anti-aircraft guns. Not a light anywhere, there wasn't the tiniest crack of light to be seen anywhere'. Having returned to the flat without injury they sat at an upstairs window where 'a battery over in Hyde Park, a couple of blocks from the house' made the panes shake when it fired, with 'the pieces of shrapnel falling in the street like light hail'.

While inspection of the Underground station shelters, which was not completed until about 10.30 p.m., was going on, a force of twenty-five Gothas and two Giants had been despatched and ordered to attack London. In the event, only three Gothas reached the metropolis. This was a miserable showing from an enemy viewpoint, considering that the attack had been intended as the heaviest on the capital to date by aeroplanes. However, it was the weather, not London's anti-aircraft defences, that undermined the raid, with significant cloud cover in places reaching an altitude of 7,000ft forming above the south-east of England. It was not to prove a good night for the bombers, with six Gothas lost, all in crashes when attempting to land back at continental bases.

High-explosive and incendiary bombs or not, there is no question that night attacks by aeroplanes placed unforeseen demands on the civilian population. When an attack was expected, buses would cease running, line up in the middle of the wider streets and extinguish their lights, taxis would cease to offer service (as Grider and his party discovered), and many of the trains on the 'tube' system stopped running.

Left: 61 Farringdon Road was
damaged by one of the fifteen
High Explosive and fifty-five
incendiaries dropped by Zeppelin
L13 (Kapitanleut Mathy) on
the night of 8 September 1915.
(Author)

Below: This commemorative plaque
on the building was photographed
about 1980. (Author)

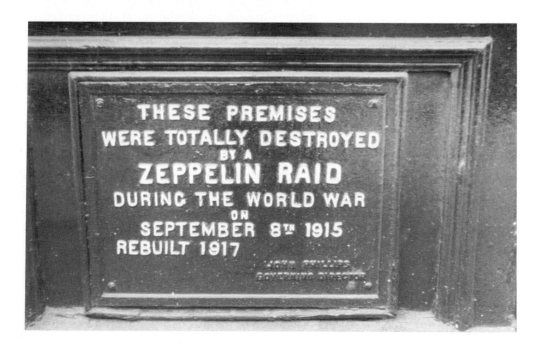

Light anti-aircraft gun of the First World War period. (Courtesy Croydon Airport Society)

London's Underground continued to provide shelter, however, despite growing problems associated with the spread of lice and typhoid fever. Much of the system's attraction was due to the complete escape from the noise of air attacks which it offered and as late as February 1918 it was announced that a third of a million people made use of the shelter it provided – a higher figure than any recorded for the Blitz of twenty-two years later. People continued to rush to the stations despite the foul conditions and an unsanitary stench resulting from the mixture of dust, human excreta and sweat.

Although these conditions were prevalent, there were exceptions, South Kensington Station being one. This was perhaps due in part to the fact that the Piccadilly section of this station had been opened as recently as August 1907. A report appeared praising the order and cleanliness here, detailing how the children were laid out in two rows with a passage between, adults being expected to do so too, since it was found that if people were allowed to walk about they were inclined to make a rush at any unusual sound. It is charitable to assume that it was this shelter to which the Home Secretary referred in answer to a question in the House of Commons on 21 February 1918 about the very real dangers of the spreading of disease within the Tube shelters. He claimed: 'The Tubes are thoroughly cleansed and disinfected by the management before traffic is resumed'.

Additionally, the introduction of chairs or boxes was forbidden. It is also interesting to note that two constables of especially formidable physique were regularly on duty at the top of station stairs to 'regulate the torrent of men, women and children which poured in'.

It is important to remember that, even in the atmosphere of sanctuary offered by the stations, the horrors of the battlefront were not far distant. Returning soldiers brought these horrors home, and the shelter of the stations was not always a comfort. A first-aid worker at Earl's Court recalled the case of a young soldier who had returned to 'Blighty' with a serious head wound, and constantly fell victim to bouts of breathlessness and violence, imagining himself still in France and going 'over the top'. Attempts to reduce his temperature with wet towels served to revive him, but also to increase his terror, as he imagined that the moisture he felt on his face was in fact blood, and therefore endured again the feelings that his wound had engendered.

Underground stations were not the only form of shelter open to the public during the war years. In the Poplar district of London, where warning of an attack was given by hand-held rattles, the Blackwall Tunnel was used as a shelter. Elsewhere, resort was made to natural caves, that part of the Kent coast

A group of shelterers in Dover's Oil Mills Cave in 1916. (Alfred Leney collection)

The vaults beneath the Phoenix Brewery provided shelter for this crowd of people during an air raid. (Alfred Leney collection)

which is predominantly chalky being especially suitable. The caves excavated behind the old Oil Mills in Dover's Snargate Street were typical, and penetrated to a considerable distance through the chalk, back into the rising ground behind. They were also lofty, well-ventilated chambers with several entrances. Wooden benches were fastened along the walls, and separate caverns designated for males and females. The crowds which assembled each night to await the hour of opening were kept under control by soldiers from the former factory nearby, which was now used as a rest barracks. These men were augmented by civilian volunteers. The caves in Trevanion Street were similarly pressed into use as shelters.

Additionally, following London's example, substantial buildings were thrown open as refuges. These included the crypt under Dover's ancient Town Hall, which had a maximum capacity of 800 persons, while six cells and passages of the police station also offered sanctuary for 800 persons. The Muster Room, like the remainder of the building, with its windows heavily protected by sandbags, was reserved for the elderly. Special arrangements were made for infants and their mothers in the former Saddle Room. The cellars of Alfred Leney's Phoenix Brewery also provided refuge, as did the tunnel in the Western Heights, and most locations were fitted out with benches and equipped with electric lighting.

A motor lorry is stopped and the driver's papers examined on a check point on a trunk road out of Dover. (Alfred Leney collection)

Inevitably, human nature being what it is, people found humour in their predicament. Many were amused by stories such as that recorded by an author,[*] writing eighteen months after the event, of a poacher who fled, leaving his tackle behind, when an enemy bomb exploded in the wood where he was setting his traps. The man immediately reported the incident to the police without realising that, by doing so, he was incriminating himself. The authorities, we are assured, 'took a sportsman-like view of the matter' and no 'proceedings' followed.

There were more serious issues, quite unconnected to actual enemy action, affecting life 'above ground' during the war years. As well as the dangers associated with the reduction in lighting, an issue which was of great and immediate concern to both Church and government was the rise of prostitution in towns. In an attempt to curb the increase, the government looked to a little-remembered provision of the Defence of the Realm Act, Regulation 40d, which stated that 'A woman having Syphillis, Gonorrhoea or Soft Cahncre' was likely to be arrested after having had sexual intercourse with any member of the Armed Forces and 'remanded in Custody for a period not less than one week and duly examined for Venereal Disease'.

---

[*] *Dover and the Great War* by J.B. Firth.

Although Grider described his female friends and those of his colleagues as 'good-sports, good-looking and well-educated' who did not 'sit around and worry about their honour all the time', adding that the men he knew would have nothing to do with anyone, male or female, who expected to 'indulge in any horizontal refreshment', there were others who were less fastidious, taking refuge in the knowledge that public attitudes of the time preferred to ignore the existence of the 'VD' menace. The problem was thought to have been adequately dealt with by the provisions of the Contagious Diseases Act, which had been drawn up as early as 1864, in order to monitor the activities of prostitutes in garrison towns such as Woolwich and Windsor, where syphilis was rife. This stated that suspect women could be taken at random from the streets and subjected to a degrading examination. Refusal to undergo this examination would result almost certainly in imprisonment. Although the Act was repealed twenty-two years later it continued to colour official thinking.

The Bishop of London, who was alive to the problems associated with this inadequate and unjust law even before the introduction of a Parliamentary Bill to raise the age of consent (then standing at between thirteen and sixteen) to between sixteen and eighteen years of age, leaves an unsavoury description of London in his book *Clean Up London*, published in 1915: 'For instance what are we to say to the male hawks who walk up and down this very Piccadilly night by night with twenty of thirty helpless and trembling girls under their surveillance, and who take from them the very money they earn by their shame. I am not a blood-thirsty man, but say that shooting is too good for them'.

The following year it was announced that there were already more than 50,000 cases of syphilis among British servicemen. There was a frequently repeated allegation that a high percentage of soldiers housed in the new wings of Epsom Grandstand, which had been adapted for use as a temporary military hospital, were suffering from venereal disease, but this is discounted by modern historians. However, the problem was still considered sufficiently real and dangerous for it to be deemed necessary to set up a Royal Commission in order to look into the problem. The issue was not only pervading the city streets but the communities created in the new shelters.

The so-called 'Tilbury' shelter was to gain special notoriety. The shelter was, in fact, situated at Stepney, where it is said some 19,000 persons could find sanctuary in the veritable 'rabbit warren' of vaults beneath the railway. Only about a sixth of this total could cram into the reinforced section, and the protection offered in the remainder was therefore more psychological than actual.

Although the pressures of the war years created some sense of unity, there was a certain cynical side to society that was always present. Subtle profiteers saw opportunity in war, making money from the vulnerable bereaved, charging high prices for 'memoriam pendants containing a portrait or hair and regimental crest' of a deceased loved-one. These lockets could be purchased with 15 carat gold embellishments for £4 10s each. In addition, war memorial tablets in stone or bronze were advertised as being available for erection inside churches, costing from £5. These also sold well.

To signify increasing losses in France, memorial plaques appeared in parish churches at home. This one in Somerset records the death of Lt Philip Worsley Battersby whose DH4 A7493 was shot down by Oblt Ritter von Dostler at about 10.30 a.m. near Lille on 7 July 1917. (Author's collection)

Other Problems

The social changes brought about by the war created a sense of unease in the population. When the rationing of foodstuffs was introduced later on, it offered a kind of safety valve for public discontent. And with the lengthening lists of casualties in local newspapers, the increasingly common sight of convoys of Ford Model 'T' ambulances bringing the 'lucky' warriors home, and the large number of men in 'hospital blues' in the streets – convalescent (but all too often mutilated) service men identified by vivid blue jacket and trousers, white shirt and red tie – hopes of a quick victory on the continent were fading, leaving those in Britain struggling to comprehend not only a new way of life at home, but the huge challenges facing the soldiers fighting abroad.

SIX

AN END OF THE OLD WORLD

Though the public was to become well-acquainted with the 'blackout' during the Second World War, the citizens of two decades earlier were not as familiar with what was called at the time the 'darkening of the lights' or 'dimout'; one contemporary writer gently admonished any readers who were careless with their curtaining, pointing out that 'a Zeppelin crew can see the back of a house as well as the front'.

The decision to reduce any public or private illumination visible externally was officially taken under Section 11 of the Defence of the Realm (Consolidation) Regulations of 1914, and the rules became law on Friday 1 October 1915.

The law was applicable to the 700sq. miles under the care of the Metropolitan Police. The area extended 15 miles from Charing Cross, spreading north as far as Cheshunt, to Epsom in the south and east, and west to Dartmouth and Staines respectively. The City of London and Birmingham had announced similar regulations on 23 November 1914.

Action on reducing the light visible in urban areas was long overdue; Kpt-lt Linnarz described a flight of 31 May 1915, during which he saw 'the lights of Ipswich'. The ocean of light that he spotted was in fact Shoeburyness, where he had arrived following a navigational error, but his observation serves to underline the vulnerability of a well-lit town to hostile aircraft.

The new law was seemingly straightforward, simply requiring that 'all bright lights be shaded'. Office windows should be covered with brown paper and blinds and curtains drawn at a predetermined time. The use of powerful headlamps on motor vehicles was banned. Enforcement of this last regulation was to create problems; even nineteen months later, in April 1917, London's police were requesting that the Automobile Association, itself an organisation founded only twelve years before, order its patrols to stop drivers who flouted the lighting regulations and to remind them of the law's requirements, including the fact

Postcard from a Croydon resident mentioning 'a lot of damage' there, a reference to the attack at about 11.20 p.m. by L14 (Kptlt Bocker), causing severe damage to houses in Beech House, Edridge and Oval Roads on 13 October 1915. (Author's collection)

that clusters of headlamps were banned. Only a single light was now tolerated, although a pair of reduced intensity was preferred with a red rear lamp.

The lighting requirements for public service vehicles were no less stringent, and covered trains, buses and trams (the latter being at first limited to a speed of 6mph). Reduction of internal illumination in all three modes of transport was achieved by drawing blinds over windows. This was simple with regard to trams, some of the older specimens retaining curtains as a standard fitting. Bus headlamps had to be partially obscured with black paint. In some areas tram headlights were obscured with masks which displayed the destination by way of a one or two-letter code cut in the material, allowing the light to show through.

Measures such as these were introduced before the adoption of the first Daylight Saving Scheme. When the scheme was finally introduced, it did little for shopkeepers, who were already obliged to reduce their window lighting from 6 p.m. each night. This was difficult, particularly in winter, and it was not unusual for windows to contain a placard advising 'See This Display in Daylight'. It was proposed that instead of keeping to the traditional closing time of 7.30 p.m., shops might do so instead at 6 p.m. The number of naptha flares in street markets also had to be reduced.

In London, especially, the multitude of decorative street lamps were to pose special problems, it becoming customary to light only one bulb or jet among clusters, while others were totally extinguished. Ordinary street lamps were dimmed or, as was the case at Princes Gate SW, only every alternate lamp was lit. Ultimately, in the words of one contemporary writer, 'pavements [were] reduced to a series of pools of light, each lamp throwing a circle of illumination about 3 yards in diameter carved out of the night upon the ground and no rays whatever thrown upwards', so that 'streets were tunnels of blackness on moonless winter nights'. Pedestrians found pathways difficult to negotiate on routes where the policy was to light only every third or fourth lamp.

Additionally, a scheme was proposed whereby parks were softly illuminated in order to create a uniformity with nearby towns, as it was discovered that the 'pools of blackness' which parks created could be identified by aircraft and used to set even a dimly lit town in sharp contrast.

Under such conditions it came as a relief when 'hand electric flash lamps of low power' were permitted and measures were taken to whiten kerbs and so on. The final judgement on the new measures, however, had to be made from the air and, describing his interception of an enemy airship on the night of 13 October 1915 – twelve days after the lighting restrictions had been introduced – eighteen-year-old Second Lieutenant Slessor wrote that 'the lights of the capital presented a wonderful spectacle. They did more. They illuminated quite effectively the great silver shape of Zeppelin L15, clearly visible in the glow from the lights of London'.

If the lighting restrictions imposed on the metropolis seemed severe, they were relatively tame compared with those introduced in various other regions. A notable example was the east-coast town which suffered a complete blackout after sunset, a town where not even shaded lights were tolerated. Similar restrictions were simultaneously imposed in Cromer and King's Lynn among others. Outside London, lighting regulations were drawn up on a local basis and, as a consequence, varied greatly. The absurdity that could arise from this state of affairs is illustrated by the fact that residents from a Hampshire town, where rules were moderate, could look towards their neighbouring conurbation and be confronted with 'a blaze of light', the nearby settlement falling under the jurisdiction of Dorset, which had different ideas! Like London, this area demanded only a reduction in lighting, although, since it was on the south coast, regulations were strictly enforced, windows being expected to be covered with curtains or blinds, street lamps having to be 'blued', and the headlamps of buses covered by black and white celluloid discs while those of trams were obscured by black paint.

Inside these vehicles, light fittings were covered with blue globes. Even these lights were extinguished on a particular route which ran beside open country and was visible from the sea, as a precaution against 'lurking submarines'. Conductors on the route had to collect fares by torchlight, particularly on the open top decks.

This district was also among those which maintained a policy of reducing both electricity and gas pressure if warning of a potential attack was received. Both supplies were cut off if an attack materialised, thus plunging the area into blackness. In London, too, a similar policy had been adopted by September 1916. The effectiveness of the measure was confirmed by Kpt-lt H. von Buttlar, who was commanding L30 as part of an airship attack: 'That night at 12 o'clock I was over London [and] underneath us every spark of light went out. How magnificently their 'lights out' orders functioned!'

Public clocks, even including Big Ben, had their chimes silenced throughout the war years, though for some this was only between dawn and dusk. Some areas suspended public transport after 10 p.m. to reduce fuel consumption. Trams were especially profligate users of electricity, and at least one local authority, obedient to the Government's plea to conserve energy, marked tram standards supporting the overhead wires with a series of coloured circles to indicate to drivers where it was safe to cut off power and allow their vehicle to freewheel, traffic conditions permitting.

Most irritations caused by the lighting regulations were cheerfully accepted but, due to forgetfulness, carelessness or even, on occasion, deliberate and foolish defiance, a steady stream of cases of lights being unscreened were brought before the courts. The resultant fines were generally in the region of £5, a sum then much more substantial than it sounds today. Today, we can get an idea of the severity of the fine if we observe that the price of letter postage in 1915 was one penny, while a stamp for a postcard was half that sum.

There were other irritations unconnected with lighting restrictions, such as the banning of whistling for taxis between the hours of 10 p.m. and 7 a.m., which came into effect on Monday 12 August.

It is unusual for young persons to fail to take in their stride whatever life, and their elders, care to fling at them, but for those of more mature years such equanimity is uncommon. The government's first steps to enumerate and award state identification to civilians under the National Registration Act of 1915 came as something of a shock when it was approved by Parliament on 14 July. The actual National Registration Day came about one month later, on 15 August. The net was cast widely and all civilians of both sexes between the ages of fifteen and sixty-five were registered. War or no war, some thought that this was foreign to their way of life, an un–British concept quite different from the four-yearly census procedures which had been introduced in 1801.

The new Act required the issuing of a personal identity certificate to each adult, which was no more than a piece of folded buff-coloured card measuring 3⅛in (80mm) by 4⅝in (117mm), and smaller than those issued in 1939. Inside these new cards was the surname of the holder, and the Christian name by which they were generally known (ignoring any others, even by initial), their occupation and address, a space for the individual's signature, and the all-important official stamp.

One other civilian card was to appear during the years of the First World War, this being issued to those on work of national importance. These cards stated the holder's name, employer, War Service Badge number, age, private address and the date of issue. On the reverse of these white cards was an intimidating list headed 'Heavy Penalties', describing the likely punishments following conviction for improper use.

Among the many, largely forgotten, uniformed civilian services which sprang up after the declaration of war in 1914 were the Women's Patrols, introduced by the National Union of Women Workers in February 1915, being given the responsibility, as one contemporary description ran, of 'safeguarding the welfare of girls from the dangers and temptations of a town which has [stationed in it] a large number of troops'.

Members of these patrols were normally unpaid, and local patrol strengths were small, the average-sized town having a force of about forty who patrolled in pairs for two spells of evening duty, each of two hours' duration. London, an exception, mustered a total of 5,842 patrol members, and it was here that they quickly became popular, earning the unofficial name of 'girls' friends'. Uniform consisted of a dark blue tunic, single-breasted with three dark buttons, a belt of the same material and a long skirt, all topped with a wide-brimmed matching hat with a silver badge bearing the letters NUWW. The shirt was white with a black masculine-looking tie, and patrol leaders were identified by two silver, five-pointed stars worn horizontally on the left lapel of the jacket. Each of these ladies, although having no powers of arrest, carried a whistle on a chain in their upper, left-hand pocket, in the manner of the police. Above the left cuff was a police-style blue and white vertically striped brassard, which surrounded a metal, shield-shaped badge similar to that on the hat, but with the addition of their registered number. White gloves were worn and a candle-lantern carried, as was an authorisation card, which in London was signed by the Commissioner of the Metropolitan Police, Sir Edward Henry, and in other districts by the Chief Constable.

Training was based on a policy of tactful preventative welfare on beats prescribed by the local constabulary, and their work is described as having largely achieved its aims. The success of the patrols also resulted in the foundation of the Empire Clubs for girls, where the activities included Swedish drill (similar to today's aerobics), physical training (PE), class singing and dressmaking.

Between January 1917 and the following September, duty times for some patrol members were extended to three hours instead of two, members now being paid at standard police rates. In June it is recorded that four ladies had been specially trained to perform seven-hour turns of duty.

The post-war use of women police on a regular footing (a small volunteer force of women police had even existed in London in 1914), meant that, with effect from 30 September 1919, the patrols were disbanded. One hundred policewomen had been recruited from the earlier patrols, and this was an impressive testimony to the organisation when it is remembered that, at this date, the total strength of the Metropolitan women police was no more than 150. It was left to one contemporary writer to point out that there was no longer any use for more than one women's force, although the work of each was not completely similar.

It is seldom realised that a third organisation, known as the Women's Police Service, headed by a Miss Damer-Dawson, had been established by a group of Chelsea ladies as a result of their 'concern for Belgian refugees'. This service was never popular with the wider public as it was regarded as consisting of 'eccentrics and feminists', with a strong ex-Suffragette element in their ranks. Soon after the Armistice the service was prosecuted under the Police Act of 1919, charged with allowing its members to 'wear a uniform resembling that of a police officer'. The dress was subsequently modified, the name being changed to the 'Auxiliary Women's Police', but in time the organisation gradually faded away.

When the Allies declared war on the Kaiser's Germany, one of the most immediate and obvious signs of change was the commandeering of around 300 buses to be used for troop transport. As a consequence, there was a huge demand for male volunteer drivers, and the massive influx that followed consisted largely of men who had been driving the same buses along the streets only weeks before. It is interesting to note also that there was no chance of these vehicles being replaced, since the principal builder of the capital's buses, AEC (Associated Equipment Company) was now concentrating almost solely on the production of military vehicles.

The shortage of personnel was solved in a manner soon to be adopted by the fighting services, namely by the adoption of female labour. In the event, this was to meet with unexpected opposition from the trade unions, until agreement was reached in March 1915 that female recruits would be regarded as 'temporary women substitutes'.

Despite wartime demands, the programme of steady improvement to the Underground system still went ahead, and the Bakerloo Line, the subject of an extension northwards since 1913, provided a unique chance for female tube staff to vindicate themselves when the new Maida Vale Station was opened on 6 June 1915. The station was staffed entirely by women. Five months later the first bus conductresses appeared on Thomas Tilling's Route 37, while the London General Omnibus Co. opened a training school for the new intake at Chelsea.

Thus was established a public transport policy which was to be emulated throughout the country. A few areas adopted an alternative system, employing young lads under military age, but this may well have been an economy measure, since their wages were less than that of their adult female counterparts elsewhere, who usually received pay equal to that of men.

The outbreak of war against the Kaiser's Germany did not require any new special force of police to be created, as the passing of the Special Constables Act in 1831 meant that there were already 'Specials' available to come to the fore in assisting the permanent police. There existed for this force a number of awards, aimed at maintaining efficiency and encouraging enthusiasm, and ultimately including Long Service Badges, Certificates for Drill Efficiency, and Ambulance and First Aid Qualifications. Some regions even had a small corps of buglers to augment the Boy Scouts in sounding the 'All Clear' at the end of an air attack, as well as Motor Sections, often driving vehicles voluntarily donated by wealthy citizens. The Metropolitan area had a complete section formed from members whose normal work was that of Automobile Association Scouts (Patrols) and in 1916–17, when motor taxation had been increased to remedy the deterioration of road surfaces, this section was described as being every night 'on duty with machines lined up and ready'. Indeed, the only branch of the Specials exempt from normal police work were those who were simultaneously members of the Metropolitan Observer Corps.

The long hours which Special Constables devoted to their duties, in addition to their normal, full-time jobs, is perhaps best illustrated by the case of Inspector Gale of 'Z' Division who, over a period of four years ending on 16 August 1918, had amassed a total of 1,513 hours, the fraction being accounted for by the rule that a drill period equalled half of one devoted to 'duty'. The relatively swift turnaround of personnel evident from surviving records was due to members of the Special Constabulary being in no way exempt from service in the armed forces if of military age.

The impact of war on Britain's civilians had, until 1914, always been slight, the slow communications via which news of events reached the public reducing the impact of events which may have taken place months earlier. All previous conflicts had been fought by the country's small, professional army, so that news of events in the Boer War, which had ended two years before the European conflict, such as the news that Mafeking had finally been relieved, was not celebrated at home until some time after the event.

In August 1914 a part of Britain's Army had been sent to France as the British Expeditionary Force. The force numbered less than 100,000 men, and it was not long before impassioned appeals for recruits were being made as it became clear that Germany was unlikely to be beaten 'by Christmas', the optimistic target that had been set as the war began. That the Army was struggling is little surprise, given that Britain's politicians had, inevitably, remained in ignorance of the fact that the Army was numerically incapable of waging war in continental Europe, its strength, without reservists, totalling only 247,432 officers and men, with some

8,000 of these being in India at the time. The scale of the issue was highlighted when, in March 1915, Kitchener estimated that an Army of 1,000,000 men was required. One of the first schemes aimed at recruiting this number was suggested by Lord Derby, appointed Director of Recruitment in September, but few at the time realised that failure to fulfil the project's aims would result in conscription.

The Derby Scheme, as it quickly became known, required that young men who were already recorded on the National Register of that August would attest their readiness for military service. Details of males aged between sixteen and sixty-five years of age were forwarded to the commanding officer of their local recruitment area, the attestations having been divided into forty-six categories of which the first twenty-three listed unmarried men, sub-divided into age groups between eighteen and forty. None were necessarily called to the colours at once, but were, in the meantime, identified by a khaki armlet bearing a red crown in its centre, which was to be worn with their civilian clothing.

In order to publicise the Derby Scheme, parades and demonstrations were organised at a local level, one town in the South East proudly boasting that, as a result of the personal appearance of a number of ex-servicemen who had fought in the Crimean war sixty-one years before, 10,000 men had volunteered.

November 1915 saw the nationwide creation of local tribunals to hear claims of potential hardship likely to be suffered by the dependants of volunteers. Success in mitigating these varied as a result of differing standards being adopted. In general, tribunals were expected to balance the demands of the armed forces against those of industry, as well as looking into likely domestic, business or financial hardship. There were allegations that right of appeal was more readily granted if it seemed a man was indispensable to his employer, rather than for any other reason.

By the beginning of 1916 it was clear that the Derby Scheme would fail, and the Military Service Bill was placed before Parliament on 5 January to introduce conscription of young men. Before it became law on 10 February, there was bitter and sustained opposition from some quarters, the 'serious differences of opinion' being described as 'so grave as to threaten the break up of the Cabinet'. It was added that 'the collapse of the Government at this moment would be a grave national disaster' which would, said Lord Lansdowne 'be of the utmost encouragement to our foes'. That opposition to the Bill crossed social barriers is indicated by a handbill issued by a North London workers' group:

DOWN WITH CONSCRIPTION!
RESIST PRUSSIANISM!
Men and Women Workers:
The Government are conspiring to rob you of what little Freedom you have left. The Defence of the Realm Act deprived you of the legal right to get better wages or even to leave your employer for a better job.
    Your brothers, your sisters, your sweethearts have shed their blood, as they supposed, to protect your liberties and crush Prussian militarism. Your leaders are now trying to crush yours with British militarism.

In South Wales, on the Clyde and in many other places discontent is rampant among your fellow workers, but the Government will not allow the Press to give you the facts.

Now they are demanding Conscription so as to put the chain more tightly on your necks. They do not want Conscription so much to end the war as to make workshop slaves of you by putting you under military control.

This will rob you of your last remnant of freedom. To prevent this you must act at once, be fearless in opposing it, you will not stand alone as the great mass of workers are ready to resist!

DOWN WITH CONSCRIPTION!
Married or single, attached or unattached,
if the Conscription Service Bill becomes law:
DOWN TOOLS!

Nevertheless, conscription became law and immediately spawned a rash of new military tribunals to hear the pleas of those who were opposed to killing fellow men for a variety of reasons. Although a flood of self-congratulatory reports by these distrusted bodies were published after 1918, it is abundantly clear that the conscientious objectors whose cases they had to hear were considered little more than traitors by the majority. Those who were directed to the Army were made to perform non-combatant duties such as cookhouse work and cleaning fatigues, and were subjected to frequent indignities. At times they were even kept under armed guard, and were generally treated like criminals and prisoners. One tale exists about a number of men sent to the Front for allegedly non-combatant duties only to be court-marshalled and condemned to be shot when they refused to carry them out. In fact this was part of a wider scheme intended to frighten men who were prospective conscientious objectors, the condemned men being quietly 'pardoned' in the meantime.

Actions of this nature only served to strengthen the anti-war resolve of the North London Herald League which had been created by the left-wing Daily Herald in 1913. The movement was strengthened by the East London Federation of Suffragettes, the Workers' Socialist Federation, The Brotherhood 'Church', The Industrial Workers of the World and the No-Conscription Fellowship, to name only a few. Most of these organisations flourished in North and East London but some had a wider, national influence and held extreme socialist and Trotsky-Leninist views. They were also allegedly capable of bitter rioting between rival factions. It is said both men and women proved capable of committing hideous cruelties in cold blood on those holding opposing, and equally extreme, views.

In an early attempt to soften the 'indignity' of threatened conscription, Mrs E. Cunliffe-Owen had, in 1914, suggested the formation of what were to become known as 'Sportsmen's Battalions', which were formed from men aged between nineteen and forty-five years of age who 'by reason of their lives as sportsmen were fit and hard'. Initial training for 'Stockbrokers and City men from upper and middle classes' was carried out at Grey Towers, a mansion at Horsham, Sussex.

This Halberestadt DIII had been flown by Uffz. Heinrich Schneider of Jasta 30 until it was shot down by anti-aircraft fire on 15 February 1917. Captured intact, D234/16 was flight-tested by the RFC and to stimulate War Savings was eventually exhibited, as shown, in the Lord Mayor's procession of November in the same year. (Author)

Another similar attempt to increase the speed of recruitment was to be rooted in a sense of local loyalty; Pals Battalions were created, and the units were sometimes even paid for by the local district. Alas, this desperate attempt to find more men resulted in complete formations of 'pals' being decimated in the early battles of the Somme, plunging whole areas at home into mourning. The system failed to prove the collective panacea which its architects had hoped. Before, and even after, the introduction of conscription, a scheme was introduced whereby pairs of sergeants would prowl the streets seeking likely 'candidates' for recruitment. If the men were persuaded to join the colours, the sergeants would earn a profit of 5s per head. It was a procedure not far removed from the organised press gangs of the nineteenth century.

Yet despite the vast range of measures designed to tap every source of manpower for military service, there remained a hard core of men who objected to any form of compulsory draft. National Registration was to prove inadequate, and industry was suffering, especially the manufacture of aircraft. Due to its late entry into the production field it had endured a 40 per cent dilution of its skilled workers with non-skilled labour, while at the same time losing eminently suitable men to the trenches. This state of affairs was said to be due to official policies which, according to a contemporary spokesman were overseen 'by men who have been reared in red tape and by systems which make rapid achievement impossible', adding that 'they have become as timid as chickens and as obstinate as mules'.

In an atmosphere where a 'generous' estimate claimed that a delivery of only 600 airframes had been made following a preparatory capital expenditure of over £2,000,000 and production costs of £4,000,000, something clearly had to be done, with the result that the government decided to extend its participation in the industry, which at that time involved some 1,500 firms employing almost 250,000 workers. The first step towards greater government support was the creation of three National Aircraft Factories, the deciding factor in their construction most likely being the War Office recommendation in the spring of 1917 that the strength of the Royal Flying Corps be increased by ninety-two squadrons.

The new factories were to be NAF No.1 at Waddon, near Croydon, Surrey; No.2 at Heaton Chapel, near Stockport, where a converted factory was taken over while still under construction, and No.3 at Richmond, Surrey. Work on this last was never commenced and, indeed, No.1 was alone in being established in the manner envisaged, this on an industrial site covering 240 acres east of Beddington Aerodrome and beside the rural Coldharbour Lane which ran south to the village of Purley in an area earlier reputed to be the finest corn land in the county. Construction of the new complex was entrusted to W. Cubitt & Co., and part of the £1,500,000 set aside for the triple project was earmarked for use at Waddon, a sum approximating to about £90,000,000 today.

Cubitt Street of National Aircraft Factory No.1 site at Waddon, Surrey. Buildings on the right are representative of those which covered several acres of the site. (Author)

Ambulance building of NAF No.1. Note the Red Cross in brick over the door. (Author's collection)

The first turf was cut for this huge project on 20 September 1917, and work began immediately on the fifty-eight single-storey buildings, the last being completed in the following July, giving a total floor space of 646,483sq.ft. Raw materials were delivered via a specially-laid double railway track, which terminated with a pair of sidings on site and was served by individual loading bays – a remarkable feature for the time.

As each building was completed, machinery was installed and workers were recruited. It was therefore possible to claim that production had commenced on 15 January 1918, the first aircraft produced being DH9 No.D451, one of a batch of 500 ordered, of which only 276 were delivered. Completion of the first was marked by a social occasion which had to begin at 4 p.m. due to the impossibility of blacking out the 250,000sq.ft of glass that made up the roof.

NAF No.1 was the subject of a three-day visit by Dominion Premiers and MPs on 17, 18 and 19 July but, despite good rates of pay, labour relations were in a semi-permanent state of turmoil. The problems came to a head when the Armistice on 11 November 1918 brought production to a sudden halt. When production officially ceased on 31 December, 1,500 workers, about 75 per cent of the work force, were dismissed, and pay for the remainder was cut. The result was a series of mass demonstrations in nearby Croydon, one culminating in an address by Sylvia Pankhurst, daughter of Emmeline Pankhurst, the champion of women's suffrage.

And so ended a somewhat clumsy government attempt to solve problems in aircraft production which it had itself created. An eminent writer of the day commented that the undertaking had concluded 'with notable lack of economy'. And while the bulk of the historic buildings were to survive, devoted to other uses, almost into this century, all were razed to the ground in 1999.

Although issues such as the reduction of public lighting were a serious irritation for those living in larger towns and cities, other government schemes were to affect a much greater proportion of the population. Food rationing was perhaps the most pervasive of these schemes. The fact that food shortages would become inevitable was indicated almost immediately after the outbreak of war when, in the space of three days, a 2lb loaf of bread rose firstly by a half-penny from 3p to 4p in a seventy-two hour period. It was to rise to 10p – an all-time high – in October 1916, while other price rises included those for bacon, butter, cereals, cheese, and meat, both tinned and fresh. Sugar saw the greatest increase, doubling in price. These price rises led to the Regulation of Meals Order of 1916, which presaged food rationing on a national scale. Associated shortages in the same year brought about the idea of using detergents to replace animal fats in the manufacture of soap.

One of the first results of the Order was the restriction of meals in hotels and restaurants to three courses between the hours of 6 and 9 p.m. and only two at other times. Wednesdays were designated meatless days, with potatoes restricted to Wednesdays and Fridays.

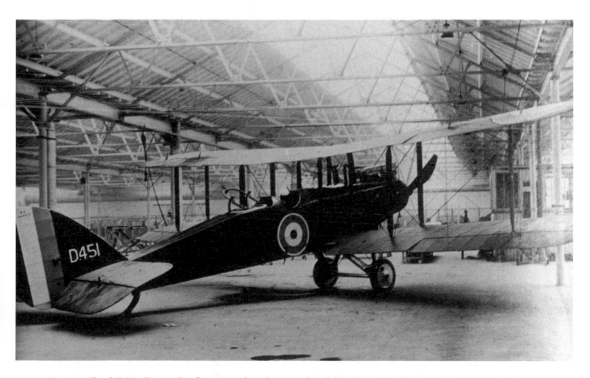

De Havilland DH9 D451, the first aircraft to be completed NAF No.1 at Waddon. (Courtesy London Borough of Sutton)

In addition to the Order, there was an attempt at introducing voluntary food rationing. In February 1917, however, the king deemed it necessary to decree that a Proclamation be read in places of worship on 6 May, urging people to consume even less meat, bread and sugar. It ran:

> ... all heads of households to reduce consumption of bread in their respective families by at least one fourth the quantity consumed in ordinary times, abstain from the use of flour in pastry, and moreover carefully to restrict or wherever possible to abandon the use thereof in all other articles than bread.

This was clearly a sign that any hopes of voluntary abstinence were fading. It therefore came as little surprise that, from 31 December, the Ministry of Food introduced what was to all intents a rationing scheme.

At first this permitted the purchase of 8oz (later 6oz) of sugar per adult, with the aid of coupons. Although the scheme was declared a success eight weeks later, it had not been without problems, chiefly due to some local authorities failing to issue the necessary dockets. More practicable ration cards were introduced with effect from 25 February 1918 for London, Middlesex, Hertfordshire, Essex, Kent, Surrey and Sussex, the rationed commodities permitting each adult only 4oz of butter or margarine, and 15oz of meat, this being extended to the whole country on 7 April. Ration books replaced the cards from 7 April, on the suggestion of Miss Emily Sidebotham of Bournemouth, customers having to register with a grocer for 4oz of fats, and a butcher for 20oz (10oz for children under ten years old) of 'meat and pork', although at first poultry, game and 5oz of bacon could be bought anywhere if a ration book was shown, although the total value was restricted to 1s 3p. Local authorities could also ration tea, jam and cheese at their discretion.

These figures make an interesting comparison with those for December 1917 when specific details were issued, under a sobering introduction which ran:

Canteen tokens for use in NAF No.1: one half penny, yellow; one penny, orange; two pence, red. (Author's collection)

RATIONING ORDER, 1918.

PASS CONTAINING LEAVE Serial R N° 026373
OR DUTY RATION BOOK. No. 9
SOLDIER OR SAILOR.

IF FOUND, RETURN TO ANY FOOD OFFICE.

No......................... Regiment...................................
Regt. No. *SOL* (Rank)....*Sgt*... (Name)....*W. Sears*.
has permission to be absent from his quarters from......*14.00 13/12/18*
to......*21.30 17/12/18*......for the purpose of proceeding to
......*London & Aldershot*
Is holder proceeding at end of leave or duty }....*n.a.*
on active service or service afloat? }
Signature and Rank }.................................. CAPTAIN.
of Officer issuing }
Sta....*BATTN.*, ...LONDON REGIMENT

N. 9a (Revised). Date..

Civilian food ration card for meat, butter and sugar. (Author's collection)

The position of the Food supply is such that the utmost economy in the use of all kinds of food must be observed by all classes and by all persons.

MEN
(Bread)
Men on very heavy industrial or on agricultural work   8lb
Men on ordinary industrial or on manual work   7lb
Men unoccupied or on sedentary work   4lb 8oz

WOMEN
(Bread)
Women on heavy industrial or agricultural work   5lb
Women on ordinary industrial work or domestic service   4lb
Women unoccupied or on sedentary work   3lb 8oz

At this time rations available to all were, per head, per week: 12oz of other cereals, 2lb of meat and 4oz of butter, margarine, lard, oils or fats. A ban on the sale of loaves less than twenty-four hours after baking existed in an attempt to prevent the purchase of more than a small number per head.

April 1918 also saw the introduction of National Food Kitchens 'for the working class population', providing low-cost take-away cooked meals. The 'kitchens' soon became 'restaurants' in which, for a price increase of 1p, 'all classes' could dine. One such 'kitchen' is recorded as having catered for 6,654 customers in its first six months, although the overall picture was disappointing; it was reported that less than 200 such 'kitchens' existed in the whole country 'due to the apathy of local authorities', according to one newspaper, all against an unofficial campaign urging the population to 'eat when you are hungry' adding that 'one meal a day would mean a big saving'. Incidentally, at about this time, unrationed horse meat became available in some areas at 1s per pound.

The early days of 1918 found Britain waging a war against grave shortages, hotels from January being prohibited from serving meat with breakfasts while 'no more that 1½oz of bread, cake, bun, scone or biscuit may be served with afternoon tea', a reduction of ½oz from the previous allowance.

Some of the districts where official food rationing had been introduced had earlier seen food riots. Even peaceable citizens were frustrated by having to endure all-day queues at the end of 1917, queues which saw children replaced by

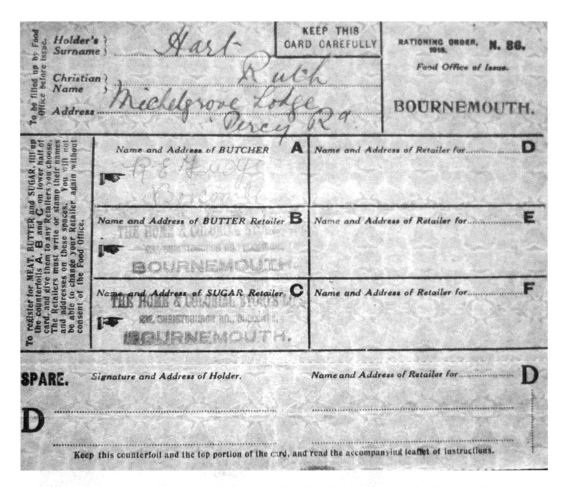

Service men on leave or on posted-out duty were issued with this food ration book. (Author's collection)

parents and in turn by grandparents in order to keep a hard-earned place in line. There would still be great demand at the end of the day if word had gone about that stocks had been delivered.

The unrest caused by such daily vigils, especially when citizens were forced to endure bad weather or if the day-long wait proved fruitless, could spill over into irrational violence, and shops owned by foreigners became targets of vandalism, especially when there even a suspicion that the owners were German.

Now, with official food rationing firmly established, severe penalties would be imposed for any breaches of the Order. Cases were publicised in order to warn the public that the regulations were strictly enforced, an example being that of a man who was fined £500 (about £30,000 in the currency of today) and imprisoned for a month for having hoarded 144lb of sugar, fourteen hams, and twenty-seven tins of foodstuffs such as sardines. Another case involved a man sentenced to three months imprisonment for 'unlawfully obtaining and using ration books'.

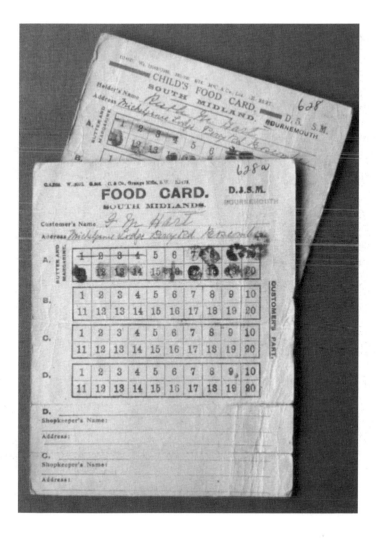

Civilian food ration cards for butter and margarine. (Author's collection)

Civilian food ration books for butter and meat. (Author's collection)

Foreground, jam spaces in a civilian ration book with a child's book in the background, the gold-lettered pouch was sold in aid of wounded horses. (Author's collection)

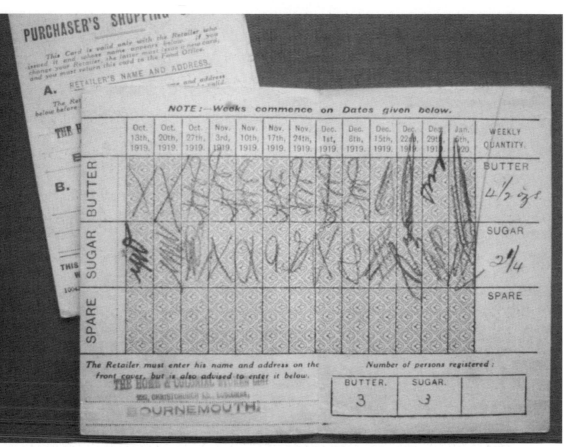

Butter and sugar page from a ration book valid for 4½oz of butter and 2¼oz of sugar per week for three persons until 6 January 1920. (Author's collection)

Such severe sentencing sent a clear message to the public that the government was serious about enforcing a system of rationing on most foodstuffs and, as Sir William Beverage was later to recall, by 1918 there existed 'control over nearly everything eaten of drunk by 40,000,000 persons'. This is perhaps an oversimplification as, in this matter as in many others during these war years, there existed significant regional variations in lifestyle. In Cardiff, for instance, the purple-veined 'horse-bean' was to become a staple part of every resident's diet for a time, yet on the other side of the British Isles the villagers of Chipstead, only 15 miles from Westminster, enjoyed a reasonably normal diet, one recalling 'We never went short of food because pigs and sheep continued to be bred and the fields were dug up to plant potatoes and other vegetables'. A sign of the times was the 1916 announcement that, from 1 May, the North Eastern Railway was, with only a few exceptions, withdrawing restaurant cars from its trains. Despite the best efforts of the authorities, however, there is no doubt that profiteering and the black market were rife.

Food was not the only commodity in short supply; shortages of petrol and coal soon arose, and these were certainly national rather than regional. The petrol famine led to the rationing of the fuel in August 1916, with costs per gallon standing at 1s 8p for First Quality and 1s 6p for Second Quality. Coal, another essential resource, was at one time in such short supply that a sharp reduction in London's Underground services resulted. Sunday services to Aldwych were abandoned after 8 April 1918, and fifteen stations were required to close at 11 p.m. from 1 May. Four days later, Sunday services were suspended to Down Street, Goodge Street, Mornington Crescent and York Road, and those to Clapham North and the Post Office were restricted to half a day on Sundays. These steps were all necessary in an effort to save the fuel-starved generators for priority week-day train services. The severity of the coal shortage was emphasised by the appearance of window cards bearing such reminders as 'Keep the home fires burning LOW then BRITISH COAL will win the war', 'Unnecessary travelling uses COAL required to warm our homes', and later, 'LESS COAL for trains at home means more ships to bring Americans'.

The sale of alcohol had been restricted by the Intoxicating Liquor (Temporary Restrictions) Order which had been introduced very early on in the war, in 1914. This restricted public house opening hours to between 8 a.m. and 9 p.m. on weekdays and 12.30 p.m. to 2.30 a.m. and 6 p.m. to 9 p.m. on Sundays. June 1915 saw an attempt to solve the problem of 'excessive drinking in munitions, transport and shipbuilding districts' through the introduction of a 'non-treating' Order which ruled that everyone must purchase his own beverage, a notice of the times running 'No Treating. Under the Defence of the Realm Act every person must pay for their own drink at the time of ordering'. In addition, March 1916 saw pub opening hours further restricted to between noon and 2.30 p.m. and 6 p.m. to 9 p.m. every day.

Clothes rationing was not to come until the Second World War, but a shortage of leather for footwear in 1917 resulted in the *Daily Mirror* championing the wearing of clogs, claiming that the case was 'really unanswerable from the point of view of utility. Clogs are cheaper and more lasting than boots and afford greater protection in cold and wet weather'.

Even paper and cardboard fell under the official eye in 1917, and announcements such as 'Owing to the Government having restricted the importation of cardboard we are unable for the present to dispatch our corsets in the usual neat cardboard boxes' were not uncommon. There was even a glass famine, and jar stickers appeared stating: 'Scarcity of Jars. Owing to the War jars are scarce. Return this jar to your Grocer who will PAY for it'.

While the prices of some foods were fixed in 1918, a quart of milk being 8*d* (4p); a tin of red salmon 2/4*d* (12p); pink salmon, 1/9*d* (9p); sardines, 10*d* (4p); baked beans, 5*d* (2p) with pork and beans costing 9p (4p). This was accompanied by such exhortations as the following:

SAVE THE FLOUR - FLOUR IS BREAD

We are short of food-ships. We only produce one-fifth of the wheat we eat. Four-fifths came to us in ships. If you take an ordinary loaf and cut it into five equal pieces only one of these pieces is made from home-grown wheat. Hundreds of ships that brought us wheat are carrying food and munitions and men to our armies and garrisons abroad, food and munitions to France and Italy, munitions to Russia. THE GERMAN SUBMARINES are doing their best to destroy the rest. Our sailors are tackling them. BACK UP OUR SAILORS BY SAVING OUR BREAD ... It must be the first effort of the wives of the rich and well to do, if the wife of every man who is making good money, to LESSEN as much as possible the amount of bread and wheat flour eaten in her house.

There soon followed the 1917 Flour and Bread Order fixing the price of 4lb loaves at 9d (4p).

SEVEN

THE TEMPO INCREASES

Public belief that the authorities were idle in protecting against aerial attack was not entirely justified, vilification of the government being based more on fear, and the destruction of a long-cherished insularity. There was, however, a failure to realise that the new threat called for new thinking, not a quality commonplace among governments.

However, there was a slow realisation in the corridors of power that in addition to opposing the intruders with artillery, the best means of combating aircraft was with other flying machines. As a result, aircraft regarded as the best available at the time were selected for the work. These aircraft also had the advantage of being available in considerable numbers, by the standards of the time.

As a result, BE2c aircraft and their derivatives were selected for interception of raiders. Despite known drawbacks to the aircraft, such as vulnerability to the weather, inherent instability and poor performance, the choice seemed to be justified when a machine of this type was instrumental in bringing down the first airship to be destroyed over Britain. Lieutenant W.L. Robinson, in BE2c No.2693, was awarded the Victoria Cross for the attack on the airship over Cuffley on the night of 3 September 1916.

Armament

Aircraft of this type, although designed for two occupants, were usually modified as single-seaters for home defence, the sole armament consisting of a Lewis gun, operated by the pilot, this firing Brock incendiary ammunition, which was

Wartime reading: *The Direct Hit*, a two-monthly magazine for members of the London Division of the
Rifle Brigade. (N.W. Cruwys' collection)

Wartime reading: *The Great War*, a periodical still using a picture of Leefe Robinson several years after his victory some years before. (Author's collection)

adopted from July 1916 after a successful demonstration the previous October. Machine gun belts were frequently filled with this ammunition combined with Pomeroy explosive bullets, which were destined to be superseded in February 1917 by the sensitive PSA MkII type.

The Brock machine gun ammunition had been designed specially for use against airships, as had another type of ammunition named after its developer, James Francis Buckingham. The difference between the two was that the former was intended to explode between the outer and inner covering of an airship, while the latter was an incendiary, phosphor-based bullet which had an annular hole, the seal of which melted on being fired, allowing the contents to leak out and take fire on contact with the air. This had been patented in January 1915 and, known as the MkVII bullet, had been immediately adopted for use against airships by the Royal Flying Corps.

Rockets represented another form of armament, and three or four Le Prieur missiles could be carried, inclined upwards at an angle of 15 degrees to the horizontal on the outer bays of a machine's interplane struts. These consisted of little more than the conventional type of rocket with a sheet-metal head mounted on a stabilizing rod. Their adoption for anti-airship work was clearly based on their effectiveness, which had been proven when attacking balloons which, like dirigibles, were filled with hydrogen. The name of these weapons was that of their designer, Lieutenant Y.P.G. Le Prieur of the French Navy.

A number of home defence BE2 aircraft were equipped with rockets in this manner, including 4112, flown by Lieutenant F. Sowrey on his mission to destroy Zeppelin L32. However, by this point, on the night of 23 September 1916, all but the brackets for the six rockets had been removed. This particular aircraft still displayed the pairs of suitably-aligned eyebolts on the struts, into which the stabilizing rods slid – a common method of fitting rockets, although some machines alternatively carried rails for the same purpose. Rockets were in fact never used in any action against airships.

Also unused in combat was the Vickers rocket gun. This weapon, designed at Crayford, was to prove even more interesting, since it consisted of little more than a tube, which was freely mounted on a pivot in the manner of a defensive machine gun and worked in the fashion of a modern bazooka, being loaded with individual rockets from the rear by the operating gunner.

There were numerous other devices for dealing with airships, not all of them being adopted, and many not even practical. The majority depended for their effectiveness either on the vast size of the target or the inflammable nature of the lifting agent.

Among these must be mentioned the Ranken Dart, devised by a Naval Engineering Lieutenant of that name and originally used exclusively by that service. Its weight was in the region of 13oz (368g) and was made up of a metal tube 5½in long (13.95cm), containing a black powder and high explosive mixture tipped with an iron point. The tail was fitted with spring-loaded vanes which opened and locked in that position as the missile pierced the airship's fabric, the same mechanism actuating a detonator rod so that the contents of the tube burst into flame, hopefully igniting the explosive gas escaping from the hole which had been made. These Ranken Darts were carried in containers of twenty-four, which could be released either individually or in groups.

Wartime reading: *The War Budget*, the issue for 9 December 1915. (Author's collection)

Even by 1917, by which time Leefe Robinson was a POW, souvenir cards portraying
the destruction of SL11 were still being sold. This one produced for Walker Harrison &
Garthwaites, biscuit manufacturers wrongly shows Robinson's aircraft as an Avro 504 instead
of a BE2c. (Author's collection)

Another device was that known as the Firey Grapnel, two of which were intended to be carried by a defending aircraft, which was expected to fly above and across an airship at right angles, trailing one of these devices in the hope that it would foul the enemy vessel's fabric, with the resultant jerk firing an explosive charge that would set light to the escaping gas.

In addition to inventions such as these, intercepting defenders were also expected to carry a number of either 20lb (9kg) Hale high-explosive bombs or 16lb (7kg) Woolwich-designed incendiary devices. Both, however, depended on the defending aircraft's ability to climb above the enemy vessel's altitude, an ability which few possessed. This factor apart, it was clear that in order to meet the airship raiders on anything approaching equal terms, fresh attention would have to be paid to the performance of intercepting aircraft, since the advantage of altitude always lay with the raiders, these having the ability to gain height with amazing speed, far beyond the climbing potential of normal aircraft, simply by jettisoning water ballast.

The RNAS had long put its faith in the Davis Recoilless Cannon, a weapon of which 2, 6 and 12-pounder versions existed by 1915, the last having a bore of 3in (7.62cm). However, these presented problems, such as the necessity for a comparatively large aircraft to carry them. In any case, although the RFC had begun to show interest in this weapon during 1916, it had by then become clear that the rifle-calibre machine gun represented the best compromise, a decision likely to have been influenced by the favourable outcome of tests, despite indications that it was almost inevitable that an aeroplane armed with this weapon was likely to be damaged by the muzzle-blast.

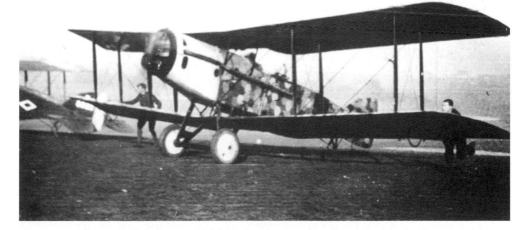

A Bristol F.2b belonging to No.141 (Home Defence) Squadron doped in a camouflage scheme strangely resembling the 'lozenge' finish common among enemy interceptors. (Author's collection)

Behold the end of a raiding " Gotha,"
A prey to Kentish fire.
Our boys at the guns have finished the Hun
And lit their funeral pyre.

A Stirring Episode in the Raid of 22nd Aug., 1917.

Left: Portrayal of a real incident. The Gotha represented having been damaged by anti-aircraft fire over Margate crashed on Hengrove golf course killing the entire crew. (Author's collection)

Below: 'A Gotha brought down in Kent' ran the official caption for this popular photograph. (Author's collection)

The wreckage of Gotha GIV 660/16 is hauled from the waters of the Thames Estuary, 5 June 1917. (Author's collection)

It was something of the proverbial 'Hobson's choice' that attempts to find an aircraft capable of meeting such a variety of differing demands were explored among modifications to the ubiquitous BE2 type. One of these variants, now largely forgotten, had undergone a change in the aerofoil, or cross-section of the wings, the first to be thus modified appearing in the early months of 1916. Although there was an improvement in the rate of climb, it was deemed insufficient. Trials continued with the standard 90hp Royal Aircraft Factory 1a motor, but this was later replaced with the 150hp Hispano-Suiza, giving a 60 per cent increase in power. This, however, although increasing the machine's performance somewhat, was still insufficient, and it was decided that a new machine should be developed around the Hispano-Suiza motor.

This was clearly a step in the right direction but, conscious that the matter was urgent, recourse was made to 'quick fix' methods, the most spectacular of which was to suspend a BE2c aircraft beneath the envelope of an SS Type non-rigid airship which would lift the aeroplane to the enemy Zeppelin's operational altitude before casting it off, hopefully to intercept the raider. Although the use of these airship-planes seemed to offer a solution to the problem, they were hastily discontinued after 21 February 1916, when the prototype was lost in a crash at the goods-yard of Strood railway station in Kent, killing occupants Commander Usborne and Lieutenant Commander Hicks. The underlying idea lingered on, however, with trials in the summer of 1918 involving a Sopwith 2F1 Camel suspended under the rigid airship R23, though the purpose of this design was in fact to provide defence for the dirigible, rather than facilitate the interception of the enemy. The purpose of single-seaters being flown off towed lighters was again quite different, these aircraft being designed to meet Zeppelins before they crossed the coast. The successful destruction of L53 by Lieutenant Culley in a Sopwith Camel on 31 July 1918 was an indication of the effectiveness of this method.

The early search for a suitable aircraft to intercept airship raiders continued in other directions, and trials by this time indicated that the best of the modifications to the BE2c airframe was that designated the BE12a, if only due to the fact that it was more manoeuvrable than those which had gone before, as well as being easier to land, an important consideration for night operations which often used rough landing grounds.

Armed with a single, fixed, forward-firing synchronised Vickers gun, the single-seat BE12a was distinguished by having biplane wings of unequal span, the upper wing measuring 40ft, and the lower shorter by 9ft 6in. The engine was a 140hp RAF 4a V12, and navigation lights, Holt landing flares and Le Prieur rockets could all be carried by this machine or its two-seat, twin-bay predecessor, the BE12. A number of both variants were issued to Home Defence Squadrons.

September 1917 was to see the introduction of yet another variant of the ubiquitous BE2 airframe, with the appearance of the BE12b. Like the BE12a it was designed from the outset as a single-seater, but retained the equal wing design of the BE2 with a new armament arrangement, consisting of a single Lewis gun firing over the upper centre-section of the wing, outside the swept arc of the airscrew.

But most important of all was the fact that the BE12b had been re-engined, now having a 200hp Hispano-Suiza V8 motor which gave a new appearance to the nose. The new car-type radiator resembled that carried by the SE5, which was also powered by a Hispano-Suiza motor. Equipment similar that fitted to the Home Defence BE12 and BE12b was carried by some, while the exhausts were occasionally flared out in shape to act as flame dampers.

Unfortunately, the type had little or no time to prove its potential for the nocturnal interception of enemy airships, since by the time that the design was finally perfected, such attacks had largely ceased. Despite this fact, the aircraft was issued to five Home Defence squadrons, though it was never to dominate any of these, being combined with FE2bs in No. 37 Squadron, BE2cs (and even a Vickers ES2) in No. 50 Squadron and with BE2es in Nos. 51, 76 and 77, the latter two even retaining some vintage BE2cs. This state of affairs typified the somewhat motley collection of aircraft retained for Home Defence, to which must be added the Avro 504K and the Vickers FB26 Vampire of 198 Depot Squadron, aircraft which, along with a few others, represented the aerial defences of these islands during 1916–17.

On 13 July, Captain Cole-Hamilton took off at the controls of one of the two Bristol Fighters sent from Northolt to intercept a formation of eighteen Gothas heading for London in daylight and, although there was a skirmish with the enemy over Ilford, neither he nor his observer were able to claim a victory.

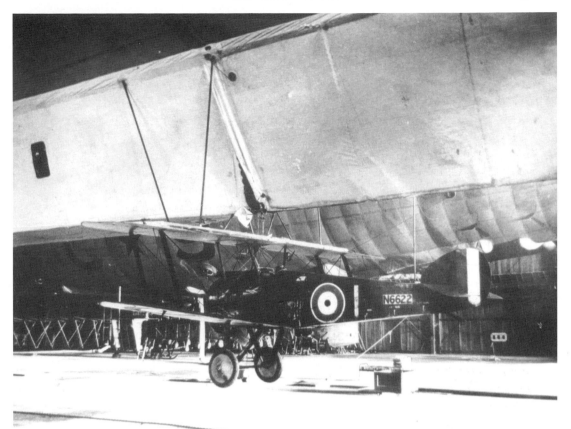

An experimental method of intercepting airship raiders was by means of a Sopwith 2F1 N6622 launched from a towed Lighter. In this way on 11 August 1918, Lt S.D. Culley brought down L53. The aircraft, here on R23s slip gar is still preserved in the IWM. (Author's collection)

Rather, this was a triumph for the raiders, since observer/gunner Captain C.H. Keevil was killed in the brief exchange of fire made as a result of the only contact with the enemy that pilots from Northolt were to have in the First World War.

These officers were serving with No.35 RS (Reserve Squadron), a training unit which had formerly been designated in common with many, as an RAS (Reserve Aeroplane Squadron), until the overall change of description which took effect from 13 January 1916. At much the same time AAPs (Aircraft Acceptance Parks) were also expected to participate in the interception of raiders. By the closing months of the war, however, much had changed, and HDs (Home Defence) Squadrons could be tabled thus for the period September–November 1918, when some standardisation of machines for Home Defence had taken place. Following is a breakdown of these in the Southern and Northern Defence Areas, a list that not only shows the areas deemed likely to be crossed by raiders, but also the near-standardisation of equipment that had been achieved by this time, the now distinctly elderly BE2 derivatives having vanished as well as the fact that the Avro 504 had now been almost entirely relegated to the North.

LONDON DEFENCE AREA

Squadron	Base	Aircraft & Notes
37	(Rochford/Stow Maries, 'A' & 'B' Flts)	Sopwith F.1 Camels
	(Goldhanger, 'C' Flt)	SE 5as
44	Hainult Farm	Sopwith F.1 Camels
50	Bekesbourne	Sopwith F.1 Camels
61	Rochford	From 2/18 SE 5as
		Later Sopwith Pups
75	(Hadleigh, 'A' Flt)	Avro 504Ks (NF)
	(Elmswell, 'B' & 'C' Flts)	
78	Sutton's Farm	20 F.1 Camels
112	Throwley	20 F.1 Camels
141	Biggin Hill	Bristol F.2bs plus Camels from 78 Squadron
143	Detling	Sopwith F.1 Camels

NORTHERN DEFENCE AREA

Squadron	Base	Aircraft & Notes
33	(Battersbey/Scampton, 'A' Flt)	
	(Kirton Lindsay, 'B' Flt)	Avro 504Ks (NF)
	(Esham 'C' Flt)	
36	(Hylton, 'A' Flt)	3 Bristols F.2bs/
	(Asgington, 'B' Flt)	3 Pups per Flt
	(Seaton Carew, 'C' Flt)	
76	(Copmanthorpe, 'A' Flt)	
	(Helperby, 'B' Flt)	Avro 504Ks (NF)
	(Catterick, 'C' Flt)	
77	(Whiteburn, 'A' Flt)	
	(Preston, 'B' Flt)	Avro 504Ks (NF)
90	(Leadenham, 'A' Flt)	
	(Buckminster, 'B' Flt)	Avro 504Ks (NF)
	(Stamford/Wittering, 'C' Flt)	

The aerodromes listed above are only a selection from a larger number, including Day Landing Grounds which existed at this time, 193 of them in the South East and Midlands, 67 in Scotland and the North East. Night Landing Grounds are not included. Additionally, it should be noted that some of the Sopwith F.1 Camels described in the list would have been those popularly described as Sopwith 'Comics', modified versions externally identifiable by having the cockpit further back than standard, and being equipped with a head-rest, with an armament consisting of twin Lewis guns on a Foster mount above the upper centre-section.

At this time also, all HD aircraft were fitted with R/T (Radio Telephones), these having the names of animals as call-signs, with related names for their bases, while patrol areas were described by geographical names. The two highest aircraft of a formation were known as 'gulls', the remainder as 'penguins'.

Listening

Despite tentative first steps being made towards a comprehensive system of tracking and control technology during the First World War, its evolution so far had been handicapped by the limited scope of the watching system on which the defences relied for their readiness. Clearly some new and giant step was necessary.

The first signs of a breakthrough came as early as the middle of 1915, and owed something to the experiments with 'listening wells' by the Army on the Western Front. These wells were excavations, at the bottom of which aircraft sounds from as much as 5 or 6 miles away could be caught, at first with the aid of a trumpet-shaped collector and stethoscope, and later with microphones. At home logical developments led to trials of acoustic reflectors, soon to be referred to as 'sound mirrors', or occasionally as 'coast watchers' or even 'track plotting mirrors'.

Much of this new science was the result of trials at the Ember Court (sometimes known as Imber Court) experimental station at Thames Ditton. A shallow, mobile, concave 'mirror', 4ft in diameter, was quickly developed and, by July, a fixed version 16ft across, had been cut in the face of the chalk cliff at Binbury Manor, Kent. Suspended a short distance from its face, a microphone was used to pick up, amplify and transmit to a listener's headphones the sounds of approaching aircraft. It was soon discovered that the hard surface gained by a rendering of cement gave even better results than the relatively soft chalk. In principle, these devices worked exactly like a modern television satellite dish.

Continued work at Ember Court and Orfordness quickly confirmed that a new era of aircraft sound location had dawned, and a large number of sound mirrors, some capable of both traverse and vertical movement, were set up along the approach routes of enemy aircraft. These were of large dimensions, their dishes being either constructed of concrete on an expanded metal and wooden frame, or excavated from the natural chalk.

An example of the later was located at Joss Gap, a short distance from North Foreland on the Kent coast. By the summer of 1918, this location had assumed increased importance due to the fact that the original dish was either replaced by or augmented by (surviving records are unclear) a sound dish, 20ft in diameter. This was pivoted from a gantry at the top of the cliff which afforded a natural shelter from the wind, and by a mounting below which permitted limited inclination. Surprisingly, the Joss Gap dish was wooden, constructed in eight sections, which were metal-braced, the timber being 3-ply, each lamination 1in thick. The front and back surfaces of the dish were separated by distance-pieces and the cavity was packed with felt. Special measures were taken to ensure that the device was camouflaged so that it was 'indistinguishable from the face of the cliff' when viewed from half a mile. Concrete, horizontal discs, level with the ground surface, were also trialled elsewhere.

Clearly the tracking of enemy aircraft by means of sound offered scope for an early warning system far in excess of that by afforded by means of sight only, and it was a logical step in the evolution of this new form of warning that, simultaneously with the perfection of sound dishes, thought was given to the question of evolving equipment for the same basic purpose as the sound mirrors but in a lighter, more portable form, capable of operation by a small body of men. The result was the sound locator.

To those familiar with the appearance of the small 'field' version of these, which was much-publicised in descriptions, photographs and film from the late 1930s, the appearance of the First World War locators will immediately be familiar, being of similar appearance, and consisting of a set of three trumpets or cones in a vertical row, balanced by a fourth on the opposite side, all mounted on a stand which could be easily moved or transported by a small group of men. The cones themselves had a mouth of about 18in diameter, tapering to an apex about 2ft behind, their construction being of sheet 'tin' giving a cross-section of a sixteen-sided polygon, since it was made up of a series of narrow, flat surfaces. The frame on which these four cones were mounted was capable of both horizontal and vertical movement so that exact bearings could be taken on the direction of the sound which the operators heard via earpieces connected to the trumpets by flexible tubes, three trumpet sizes being in existence. The first use of such locators was to give warning of approaching Gothas flying at perhaps 8,000ft, an altitude which had been indicated in the initial trials when Royal Flying Corps machines of various types had been used to test the apparatus.

However, as with the sound mirrors, problems were encountered with sound distortion created by the wind. An attempt to solve this was made by lagging the trumpets of post-1918 locators. In fact, extraneous noises were only too efficiently eliminated, but the trials were regarded as a failure since the quality of the received signals was also affected. It was not until box-like 'sheaths' were introduced, with the trumpets mounted by their rims alone, that such protective boxes became standard in the early post-war years. Interestingly, as the war drew towards its close, sound locators were used more to direct searchlights than anti-aircraft guns.

Meanwhile, it was envisaged that the sound mirror system should extend from the West Country to the North East, with sites located half a mile apart, the very first dating from 1916, and usually being no more than 15ft (4.6m) in diameter, the reflective surface having a maximum depth of 3.5ft (1.06m) without the side-walls which were introduced later to eliminate extraneous sounds. The later addition of these side-walls meant that the noise of an approaching Zeppelin travelling at perhaps 70mph at 12,000ft (3,657.6m) with a 4,000lb (1,814kg) load of bombs could be picked up while still a quarter of an hour's flying time away.

These were not the only systems for gathering early warning of enemy intentions. Also in use was a system of listening stations designed to intercept wireless transmissions from airships and sea-going vessels. There were ultimately a total of thirty such 'Y' Stations, not necessarily situated on the coast, which consisted of an Operations Block covering a site measuring 58ft (17.6m) by 22ft (6.7m) with a complex of outbuildings, the whole of which was protected by a 7ft (2.14m) high fence, and within this an open area covered in barbed wire to a depth of 25ft (0.76m). Inside this was a patrol track.

Information gathered by these stations was decoded and immediately transmitted to the Admiralty at Whitehall, while there was also a Training Station at Portsmouth. Wavelengths employed by these 'Y' Stations varied between 300 and 600m, giving them a range of between 45 and 250 nautical miles, their identification being by means of a two-letter combination, either BY of BZ, with a suffix denoting the station's location, Stockton-on-Tees, for example, being BYT, the final letter denoting 'Tees'. Only Whitehall enjoyed a single letter, with 'A' representing the headquarters of the system.

Balloons

That tethered balloons had always been a danger to powered aircraft was well-known. A typical situation occurred on 31 July 1917, a day of persistent driving rain and a cloud base down to 1,000ft. Captain Walter had taken off at 6.05 a.m. to participate with four others in a concentrated ground attack. Just north of Vlamertinghe, his DH5, No.B369, collided with the cable of an unseen observation balloon, cutting off both wings on the port side, and sending it plummeting down, killing Walter in the crash. He had been born at The Parsonage, East Farleigh, Kent, on 15 August 1896 and is buried at Lijssenthoek near Poperinghe.

There was no connection with this encounter and the idea of using balloons not necessarily to bring down and destroy raiding enemy aircraft, but to force them to a higher altitude, but the tragedy unarguably made clear the dangers of balloon cables. This knowledge stimulated a number of suggestions which came almost simultaneously from several quarters in the summer of 1916, seemingly inspired by the use of single balloons to protect Venice from the attentions of Austrian bombers. These had been inspected during the same year by a senior British officer and, in the previous July, a Halifax engineer had published a twenty-seven-page pamphlet examining the idea. Lieutenant-General Jan Christian Smutts and Major-General Ashmore proposed a similar scheme.

A prototype system was taking shape at the Balloon Training Depot in Richmond Park, Surrey, during the late summer of 1917, using Cuquot-type balloons similar to those already used by the RFC. These trial balloons, however, were linked in groups of four, and it was such a set, becoming uncontrollable on a blustery September morning, which sent two men to their deaths. The trials resulted in operational balloons being flown in groups of three, these being intended to form an aerial barrier 1 mile in length, the first twenty being set up by October 1918 to protect London's North-East and Eastern districts, leaving clear corridors for patrolling fighters between these and the belt of anti-aircraft guns which now existed in a circle around the metropolis. A further ten aprons were added by the following June.

These balloons were the responsibility of three new units of the Royal Flying Corps, which were known as Balloon Apron Squadrons, their title describing the unique nature of the barrage, now consisting of three balloons linked at 500 yard intervals along a single cable, from which were suspended at 25 yard intervals eighteen weighted, lighter steel cables, each 1,000ft in length, forming the apron which gave the barrage its name. Incidentally, the explosive charges suggested by Ashmore were omitted. Each of these three-balloon curtains were at first flown at an height of 7,000ft, but this was later increased to 9,500ft. Literature of the period announced that 12,000ft was possible.

The layout of the complete barrage was roughly that of a crescent beginning at Enfield and following an arc via Tottenham, Wanstead, Barking, and Plumstead to Lewisham in the south. There were still problems; the heavy aprons could only be successfully flown in calm weather and suffered from the fact that the weight of the steel cables tended to draw the balloons together. This was a problem that the airship pioneer E.T. Willows attempted to solve when he suggested the substitution of spherical balloons.

The altitude at which these combinations were flown was chiefly intended to be one which would force bombers to gain height to pass over them, thus denying easy and accurate bomb aiming, although it is clear that it also had a psychological effect, this being confirmed by members of aircrews taken prisoner.

There exists a report, frequently repeated by post-war writers, which claims that an enemy aircraft did in fact run into a cable apron, the crew failing to realise the fact at the time, only becoming aware later that this was the cause of a wing being damaged, and explaining why the pilot suddenly experienced difficulty in controlling the aircraft, which fell 'several hundred' feet in the darkness. In a search for what actually happened, one is tempted to reconcile this tale with the report of Zeppelin-Stakken Giant, aircraft R12 (larger and capable of carrying a bomb-load greater than that of a Gotha). This craft is alleged to have hit an apron over Woolwich at fifteen minutes after midnight on 17 February 1918. The pilot, Lieutenant Gotte, with great presence of mind, shut down all six engines, before opening up the port pair to regain control. The impact tore two bombs from their racks, which fell on Woolwich. There was some damage to the leading edge of the starboard wing of the aircraft, which was discovered later. Yet despite all this, the

One of the sphinx figures on the base of Cleopatra's needle on the Embankment bears to this day signs of bomb damage on its paws. (Author's collection)

Beckenham area of Kent was hit by bombs deliberately dropped, these allegedly falling in the Shortlands district, the aircraft used being one of a dynasty, like the others of this attack force, that was larger than some of the machines in service at the beginning of the Second World War.

The complete attacking force had consisted of five aircraft, all of the 'giant' R-type, and the commanders of three of these, R25, R33 and R36 had elected to attack the secondary target of Dover due to deteriorating weather conditions, although the last may have turned back following trouble with the bomb rack. Eighteen bombs are said to have been dropped in the St Margaret's area of Dover by one of these, leaving only R13 and R39 to carry on to London, where a heavy bomb, said to have been dropped from the latter, commanded by Hauptmann Richard von Bentivegni, did extensive damage to the Royal Hospital, Chelsea.

Casualties in the early hours of that Sunday morning were recorded at the time as consisting of thirty-seven injured (including ten women) and sixteen killed,

THE GREAT
DOUBLE EVENT,
Sep. 24ᵗʰ 1916.

Even after several years, triumphant cards commemorating victory over raiders (in this case the two, L32 and L33, which occurred on 24 September 1916) remained popular and were kept in circulation possibly for their propaganda value. (Author's collection)

three of them women. Modern research, however, suggests only twelve dead and six injured. Two of the dead are known to have been Ms Coates and Ms Sugars, who were members of an hotel still-room staff, the pair being killed when they ventured outside to see what was happening, together with a companion, who was reported as being 'severely injured'.

Moments before this explosion, William Freeman, a taxi driver, had delivered a passenger to the same hotel. He was entering the refreshment room, from where he could see his vehicle. Suddenly, there was a bright flash and, 'As soon as I saw that, I fell flat on my face, and I reckon that that saved me', he afterwards stated. The hotel had been hit, bringing down several hundred-weight of granite on to Freeman's cab, which was 'smashed almost to splinters'. The blast had also killed the man he had just dropped off, as well as another man, yet strangely, as the hotel manager was later to state, 'There were no serious injuries inside'.

Elsewhere, a Mr Bannister had braved the barrage to walk home, only to be killed at his own front door when one of two bombs fell in the middle of the road, the first 'making a crater three feet deep', although the second did little damage since it dropped into soft ground.

Meanwhile, R12, its crew allegedly ignorant of its collision with the balloon apron, and having survived two encounters with BE12 night fighters from No.59 Squadron, finally reached its base at 1.25 a.m. the following day.

For a true idea of what impact news like this would have made on the British citizen of the time, it must be viewed against the day-to-day concerns of the age. Coal was still in short supply, queues for this accompanying those for food, and with a price of 34s per ton in 1915 (increased by a further 2s a month later), it was now commonplace in coastal districts to see young women beach-combing, as it were, for flammable items. Even in central London, one case is recorded of a lady touring the capital by taxi with a laundry basket, begging for a few lumps of coal each from her friends in order to provide warmth for elderly, ill mother at home.

As the conflict continued the number quantity of paperwork issued to civilians increased. An example being the small, buff-colour certificates for men, these confirmed that the bearer was registered but had not yet been called to the colours. (Author's collection)

Popularly said to be a hiding place of letters exchanged between spies were enamelled advertisement signs such as these. (Author's collection)

It is little surprise therefore that coal was rationed in the winter of 1917–18, the allowance being based on the number of rooms in a household. Three to five qualified for 2cwt, six to seven for 4cwt, and over twelve for 8cwt, while extra allowances were made for those homes containing small children, invalids or lodgers.

The spring of 1917 was also remembered for the introduction of economies in paper, large posters being banned from that time, while newspapers continued to be reduced in size as their cost rose. *The Times*, originally a half-penny per copy, rose firstly by a further half-penny and then doubled again in price. The majority of other newspapers, at first sold at a half-penny, later sold at double that figure, their columns at regular intervals being devoted to fresh outbreaks of violence against alleged German nationals. The most serious outbreak, triggered by news of the sinking of the Lusitania in 1915 by a German submarine, was unusually vicious.

The autumn of 1917 saw an appeal to knitters to produce balaclava helmets, mittens, socks, waistcoats, scarves and wide belts for men at the Front, despite a serious shortage of knitting wool. The same season also witnessed a nationwide appeal for blankets. There were other concerns, however, the most pressing of which was the rise of fortune-telling parlours and crystal gazer's rooms in Soho, London, which were quickly recognised as nothing but gambling dens. 'Bridge clubs' also attracted large numbers of young people who were driven from their homes by the lack of coal for heating, and it was believed that such 'bridge' meetings hid darker activities than the newly popular card game, existing as haunts for agents of blackmailers and the like.

EIGHT

THE HOUR AND THE MEN

The maxim that 'cometh the hour, cometh the man' could hardly be more apposite than when applied to Britain's defence against air attack in the opening years of the First World War, since it was largely due to the skill and devotion of two now almost forgotten men that the foundations of the country's new security were laid.

Senior of this pair was Admiral Sir Percy Scott, KCB, KCVO, CVO, Hon. LLD who, having retired in 1913, was suddenly recalled by the Royal Navy two years later and, at the age of fifty-seven, given responsibility for London's gun defences. He had joined the service in 1866, rising to the rank of Captain in 1898, all the time specialising in ordnance, serving on the Admiralty Committee to advise on the subject, and being responsible for the design of the carriages on which were mounted the 6in and 4.7in weapons used in South Africa, as the perfection of various appliances to improve the shooting of heavy artillery. He had also acted as sometime Inspector of Target Practice before his retirement.

The other was Lieutenant-Commander Alfred Rawlinson, a pilot since 1910 when on 5 April he had taken Certificate No.3 at the controls of a Farman biplane flying from Shellbeach, only to break an ankle in a crash at the Bournemouth meeting of 12 July in the same year. This was also the day that the Hon. Charles Rolls died at the same gathering.

Despite his interest in aviation, it was as an explosives expert that Alfred Rawlinson was to quickly gain distinction in France where, during the winter of 1914, he had been occupied in obtaining mortars from several French arsenals and, with their aid, looking into the possibility of using smokeless powder for such weapons in trench warfare, in addition to trials of modified fuses and new explosives. This was all work which brought him into close contact with a number of personalities who were soon to aid him in a special mission for which he was suddenly dispatched in the early autumn of 1915.

Lieut. F. Sowrey. D.S.O   Luff
                              Hornchurch

Like every age, that of the First World War had it public heroes, but now they were the country's defenders. This is Lt F. Sowrey who brought down Zeppelin L32. (Author's collection)

By this time, he had been returned to England in order to convalesce from wounds sustained by 'a somewhat too close acquaintance with a 'Jack Johnson'' large calibre shell. During the recovery period he was appointed to command and instruct a squadron of RNAS armoured car personnel which was then being raised.

The event that threw together Rawlinson and Cecil Grace was the attack on London by Zeppelins LZ74 and 77, accompanied by Schutte-Lanz SL12 during the night of 7/8 September 1915. Not that this was the opening attack on the capital which had first been bombed by airships almost three months before, but coming as it did after a quiet period, the public was raised to a pitch of anger with the authorities at their inability to provide any significant protection against air raids, a sentiment springing from generations of belief that Britain was an inviolate island, with its heart indestructible.

Cynics were afterwards to claim that it was a mood of fear for their own futures rather than a sense of public duty that alarmed politicians (in those days deeply

Another being Lt W.J. Tempest who destroyed Zeppelin L31. (Author's collection)

Lieut. W.J. Tempest, D.S.O.

Luff Hornchurch

respected) into uncharacteristically swift action, but it is likely that their realisation that London's defences were grossly inadequate had much to do with the huge wave of public horror, indignation and even panic. That provision for the capital's defence was nothing short of ridiculous was known only to a few, consisting as it did of four 6-pounder Hotchkiss weapons, six 1½-pound Pom-Poms (weapons of little value since their shells were unlikely to explode on contact with the fabric of an aircraft of any type) and half a dozen 3in naval guns, these being sited near Tower Bridge and in Regent's Park, representing an augmented battery, confined to only two guns until late in May.

The first part of this force was manned by Royal Marines, the remaining four by the RNVR but the personnel in charge of the other weapons were unusual in being drawn from the ranks of the Special Constabulary, now acting as part-time members of the Naval Reserve, and expected to man the guns for a period of four hours daily, reverting to their civilian occupations outside that period.

Admiral Sir Percy Scott who was in charge of London's gun defences brought to the role a vast knowledge of guns and gunnery. (Author's collection)

That the government had not been as inactive as the public believed was proven by the decision to call on Lieutenant-Commander Rawlinson who, during the winter months of his time in France, had assisted in organising the anti-aircraft defences of Paris, where he gave special attention to ammunition and gun-sights. He was working on drawings for British adaptations of these gun-sights, when he was urgently called to the Admiralty on the afternoon of 11 September, the defence of the United Kingdom being the responsibility of the Navy at that time.

He was conducted to the office of the First Lord of the Admiralty, who introduced him to Sir Percy Scott, respected for his specialist knowledge of armament and fuses, so much so that he was described by a contemporary as having a 'profound knowledge of every detail connected with gunnery'. Before the meeting broke up it was decided that, in order to base London's defences on those of Paris, Rawlinson should be authorised to go to France, where he could obtain details of the guns and ammunition then in use. It was also decided that responsibility for manning the guns and searchlights of the capital's new mobile defences would fall to men picked from the armoured car squadron which had so recently been the Lieutenant-Commander's responsibility.

An artist's impression of the use of a Sopwith Camel aircraft to scatter War Savings leaflets over Lincoln in March 1918. This is said to have realised £452,000. (Author's collection)

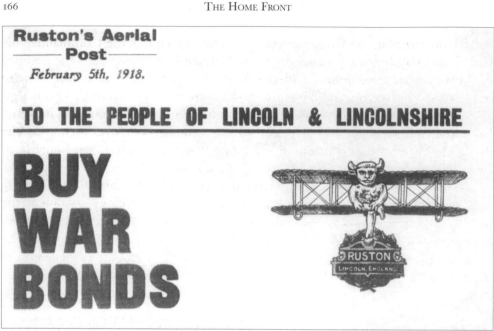

Specimen of the leaflets dropped over Lincoln. (Author's collection)

It was planned that Rawlinson would sail on 17 September but, as the date approached and the promised official letter of authorisation failed to materialise, Admiral Scott, in the best traditions of the Senior Service took it upon himself to write one personally and, armed with this, his subordinate departed by the afternoon boat from Folkestone, where the naval embarkation officer had been ordered by telegram to expedite the departure of both Rawlinson and his car. Rising early the next day, the Lieutenant-Commander set off from Boulogne en route to Paris, hopeful that an example of a 'Cannon Automobile' would be procurable. This was a 75mm auto-cannon mounted on a de Dion motorised chassis. By the greatest good luck, one such vehicle, complete with an ammunition wagon, was available on his arrival.

The next move was to visit General Clergerie, the Chief of Staff to General Gallieni, French Minister for War. A personal meeting with the visiting Englishman was planned but, at this point, Rawlinson's run of good luck finally ran out, when General Gallieni, having read Admiral Scott's letter, pointed out that only General Joffre, Commander-in-Chief of the French Army, could grant such a request.

Undaunted, Gallieni at once wrote a letter to his sixty-three-year-old superior, a status that had earned him the name of 'Papa Joffre', to the effect that the writer personally had no objection to the request for a gun of the type requested if his superior agreed. Thus equipped, Rawlinson immediately set off for the Commander's headquarters at Chantilly, some 90 miles distant, now feeling so confident of procuring a gun that he telephoned the Arsenal, requesting that a gun of the type required be made ready with all its equipment by the same evening!

Alas, on arrival at the Headquarters it was announced that the Commander-in-Chief was away, but the production of the Gallieni letter made clear the urgency of the situation. 'Papa' Joffre's Chief-of-Staff took personal responsibility for the requested authorisation, and the business was completed within half an hour, thus allowing Lieutenant-Commander Rawlinson to be away again, retracing his route back to Chantilly where he found everything ready for him, thus permitting the gun to be tested the next morning. He caught the ammunition boat home from Boulogne the same night.

The trials conducted the next day were carried out at Mount Valerien and, proving satisfactory, the weapon was prepared for the road. Together with its equipment, the device was sent ahead on its 160-mile journey to the coast, Rawlinson announcing his intention to catch up after having telegraphed from the British Embassy an order for a group of his most experienced mechanics from the armoured car squadron to meet the ammunition vessel when it docked at Newhaven that night.

Aircraft were not alone in being supported by this means. This is a similar leaflet supporting the manufacture of tanks dropped over Peterborough in February/March 1918. (Author's collection)

The trials earlier in the day had indeed proved the 75mm auto-cannon capable of the all demands placed on it. Indications were that, with an effective horizontal range of 9,500 yards and at an elevation of 50 degrees, a range of 6,000 yards at an altitude of 9,000ft was possible. At higher elevations, it was capable of throwing a shell to a height of 14,000ft. These encouraging figures continued to run in Rawlinson's head as he now gave chase to his prize which, although exceeding over five tons in weight, could easily achieve a speed in excess of 50mph, except on hills, by virtue of its 100hp motor.

Overtaking the weapon proved more difficult than anticipated and, although driving 'exceptionally fast', it was not until the car was passing through Abbeville, 50 miles short of Boulogne, that it was able to pass the speeding gun. The time was exactly 5 p.m., but it was not until midnight that the loading was complete, and the vessel with its unique cargo and an organising officer weary after an exceptionally demanding day, could cast off and set course for England.

Docking at Newhaven the following morning, where the selected men from the armoured car squadron were waiting, the gun, its ammunition wagon and the officer's car were quickly unloaded and made ready for the road. By 7 a.m. the convoy was on its way to London, this time with Rawlinson driving the mobile weapon, having already telegraphed news of his coming to Admiral Scott. A little over two hours later, all arrived safely at Sir Percy's London home. Scarcely more than three hours later, the auto-cannon had been cleaned, and was ready for the First Sea Lord's inspection on Horse Guards Parade.

During this period of intense activity Captain Stansfield and Commander Grenville Grey, both of the RNVR, had not been idle at home, taking the first steps towards the formation of the new Anti-Aircraft Defence Force, a body for which gun-positions were currently being selected and which would be responsible for both mobile and fixed weapons, as well as searchlights. The first group of guns, it was announced, would henceforth be known as the Royal Navy Anti-Aircraft Mobile Brigade, a unit which, in early October 1915, existed in little more than name, possessing the French gun as its sole armament. This was kept at the Talbot Works in Ladbroke Grove, which was also the HQ of the Armoured Car Squadron.

It appeared to the hard-working Lieutenant-Commander Rawlinson that the gun he had so recently procured would be most usefully employed in defending the City of London, since this represented a prime target for the enemy, bounded by Moorgate and Bunhill Fields and containing the Bank of England, Liverpool Street Station, Guildhall and the Bank, St Paul's and Chancery Lane Underground stations – all scarcely fifteen years old, together with that part of Moorgate Station serving the Finsbury Park Line, opened a mere eleven years before. There lay the open area associated with the Honourable Artillery Company, a centre in the City Road, only a short distance north of Moorgate, then commonly referred to as Moorgate Street.

The Honourable Artillery Company ground was associated with the oldest military body in the kingdom, which dated from 1537. The site had been home to the ancient City archery butts, where the skills of long-distance shooting were honed amongst the Finsbury fields.

All this was to be put to the test, the ground being used for a modern defensive purpose in a surprisingly short space of time. On the night of Wednesday 13 October, the enemy made his most ambitious assault yet on London.

It was only a little before 7 p.m. when Lieutenant Commander Rawlinson's telephone rang with the message that no less than five airships (L11, L13, L14, L15 and L16, all naval vessels) were expected to reach London about two hours later. The Commander was alone at the time, his men having been temporarily dismissed after an arduous day of training, and he therefore had no alternative but to prepare the equipment himself, loading the ammunition wagon and warming the vehicle's engines, having sent messengers to find as many of the scattered men as possible. By 8.25 p.m. only a few had arrived. The telephone rang once more, this time with the order that the convoy should make for the City with all speed.

Aware that the auto-cannon was the only gun available that was capable of dealing with Zeppelins, Rawlinson had an agonising wait until a sufficient number of men had arrived. The last man reported for duty at 9.04 p.m., the man being the Chief Petty Officer, an indispensable figure. One minute later the vehicles were on the road, using full headlamps and with sirens blaring* they set out with Rawlinson at the wheel of the mobile gun in the lead, making all possible speed. The civilian traffic encountered made progress difficult, becoming thicker in Oxford Street after passing Marble Arch. Despite these difficulties, however, the speedometer was registering 56mph as the vehicles swung into High Holborn, only for the leading driver to discover that the road was under repair, the area being shut off by wooden poles supported on trestles, while buses and other vehicles blocked the road to each side!

Realising that it was impossible to stop such a heavy truck at that speed, there was no alternative but to batter a way through. Thus the intrepid Rawlinson proceeded to do so, attempting to coax an even greater speed from his charge. As a blow split the first heavy pole in two, the halves spinning dangerously into the air, the steering wheel almost wrenched itself from his hands, but the gun continued to rush forward over the unmade surface, pouring out water from a split radiator. There was now the briefest second of horror as the driver realised that these was another pole obstructing his exit from the site of the excavations. He was only dimly aware of the sudden appearance of a helmetless policeman, running as only a fit man can run, his intent being to remove the new obstruction without regard to his own safety. He was successful, and at that same moment, the vehicle passed the spot, its way suddenly cleared by the policeman's efforts, the gun on its chassis bounding into the air as it passed over the pole which was even then still rolling on the ground!

---

* This gave a single rising and falling note, not the twin-pitches of the horns of emergency vehicles today.

The remainder of the journey was comparatively uneventful and, followed by the others, Rawlinson drove on to the Artillery Ground, swinging the vehicle round as he stopped, in order that the headlamps might illuminate the area where the weapon was to be set up. Scarcely had this been achieved when it became clear that a Zeppelin was approaching from the north-north-west, at about 9,000ft.

There was no time in which to range the gun accurately using instruments so, acting quickly on estimations, the officer gave the order to 'Fire' immediately on receiving the call 'Ready, sir' from the gun layer. Two rounds were fired before it became impossible to bring the gun to bear on the airship again, as the elevation was more than the maximum 83 degrees possible. However, the speed of the turn-out is indicated by the fact that the first round was fired exactly twenty minutes after the convoy had left the Talbot Works. It was later revealed that Rawlinson's second shot had been sufficiently close to the raider that water ballast and the bomb load was jettisoned in order to climb out of danger.

All this activity on the ground occurred against a background of falling bombs, which were to kill fifty-five persons and injure 114, according to the morning papers of two days later (actually seventeen had been killed and 128 hurt). Material damage amounted to £80,020, bombs having been dropped over a wide area, including London's theatreland, and even as far away as Croydon, 14 miles distant. Eighteen bombs were dropped there, where earlier a council meeting had been suspended part way through the agenda following the announcement that Zeppelins were approaching.

Although the debut of the new French gun had been inauspicious in terms of actual damage inflicted on the enemy, it was only one of twelve dedicated to London's defence, and was significant in its ushering in of a new form of defence. Almost exactly one month later, the defences had been augmented by the addition of nine mobile guns, to be sent out from the new barracks at Kenwood House, a site now associated with open-air summer orchestral concerts.

Ignorant of the new plans and the efforts being made to provide the nation with an effective system of defence, the public once more reacted angrily to the to the audacity of the latest attack. A spontaneous protest meeting, which attracted a huge number of people, was held within days at the Cannon Street Hotel. The assembled audience listened to addresses by a number of speakers demanding immediate reprisals, among them Joynson Hicks MP, who summed up the general feeling when he sneered that 'The Admiralty, after twelve months of war thought it worth while appointing someone to look after the gunnery of London. They might have appointed Sir Percy Scott a year ago'.

Clearly the nation, and Londoners in particular, had become disillusioned as the casualty figures from Neuve Chapelle, Ypres, Gallipoli and Loos mounted, forcing them to realise that war was not a great and glorious thing where Tommy Atkins carried all before him. This fact was proven by the tenor of the newspapers, which gave the scant official report of the events of 13 October beside dramatic reports of enormous British successes in France. The attack on London occupied only five column inches, running:

The popularity of photographs confirming that raiders were still being destroyed remained into the adoption of conventional aircraft to attack British targets. This is the motor and exhaust of one of the last Gotha raiders destroyed on 6 December 1918. (Author's collection)

The appended communiqué issued by the Press Bureau last evening regarding the Zeppelin raid on Wednesday night shows that 55 persons were killed, while 114 were injured. The War Office announces that a fleet of hostile airships visited eastern counties and a portion of the London area last night and dropped bombs. Anti-aircraft guns of the Royal Field Artillery attached to the Central Force were in action. An airship was seen to heel over on its side and drop to a lower altitude.

Five aeroplanes of the Royal Flying Corps went up, but owing to atmospheric conditions only one aeroplane succeeded in locating an airship. This aeroplane, however, was unable to overhaul the airship before it was lost in the fog.

Some houses were damaged and several fires started, but no serious damage was done to military material. All fires were soon brought under control by the fire brigade.

The following military casualties, in addition to the one announced last night, have been reported…

The Home Office announces the following casualties (other than the military casualties reported above):

	Men	Women	Children	Total
Killed	27	9	5	41
Injured	64	30	7	101
	91	39	12	142

Examples of the commoner interceptors used by defending pilots included this BE2e of No.100 Squadron, RFC. (Author's collection)

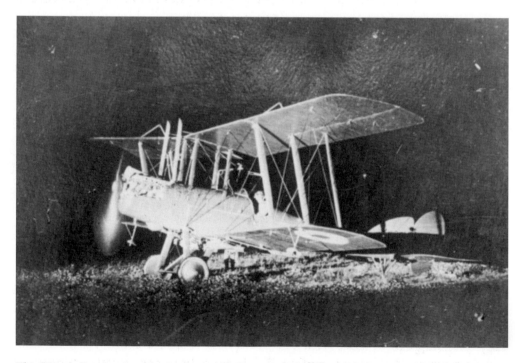

This BE12 believed to have been operated by No.12 Squadron from Cramlington was armed with rockets on the outer wing struts in addition to a forward-firing machine gun. (Author's collection)

The 'located airship' was L15, momentarily caught in searchlight beams, which attracted the attention of eighteen year old Second Lieutenant John Slessor of No.17 Squadron, flying a BE2c. This was an officer later to become Marshal of the RAF Sir John Slessor, Chief of Air Staff, thirty-five years later.

A sober analysis of the attack showed it to be one of the most successful so far, *The Sphere* at the end of 1915 stating, with surprising candour, that the total casualties up to that time were 177 killed and 384 injured. Modern research indicates that these figures erred on the conservative side, but the numbers were still sufficient at the time to keep alive the flame of public indignation, not only at the complete lack of satisfying reprisals, but also at the seeming lack of response by the defenders. The public found small crumbs of comfort in the visible activity of the searchlights, though these were, in reality, one of the weakest links in the defensive chain. Ultimately, the people looked to the guns for evidence of retaliation against the raiders, and the clear lack of sufficient artillery troubled civilians. The lack of noise from artillery was most disturbing, as people regarded a loud barrage from the guns as a satisfying indication that the defenders were giving the raiders a 'hot reception'.

The accusation of lethargy which was levelled at the government was not entirely just, however, and the augmentation of the defences with nine additional guns, all mobile, was an important step towards effective defence. The guns were crewed by sixty-three naval ratings, forty-one of them mechanics, with twenty-two ABs, and a further forty-eight detached for instruction. By the following February no less than fifty guns of several types were in reserve for the defence of the capital, with a further ninety-eight in preparation.

Production was prioritised, the figure for the 13-pounder 9cwt weapons, Types I-IV, being particularly impressive for 1916, with 234 manufactured, against a figure of only 2 in the previous year. In addition, 3in, 20cwt guns, Types I-III had also entered production, 161 being manufactured.

At the end of the year, possibly due to the deteriorating weather, which reduced the likelihood of Zeppelin attacks, it was decided that a timing exercise should be organised for the Mobile Brigade. The date chosen was three days after Christmas and, although only six guns were turned out, the details which survive are of interest as an indication of reaction times, as well as a list of the prepared sites of the time.

At each of these it was of course necessary to have access to a telephone line into which the operators could plug their standard military field telephones, giving them direct access to headquarters. Having arrived at their gun sites it was also necessary for the crews, by adherence to a strict procedure, to make their weapon ready, the process requiring men to check their telephone line, unpack and test the various instruments necessary in ranging the gun, jack up and level their weapon, and make ready the ammunition, fuses and so on. When completed, they were required to report that everything was 'ready for action'.

The warning that enemy airships had been sighted was, for the purpose of the exercise in question, regarded as having been received at Kenwood House at

6.17 p.m., and three minutes later the first mobile gun was to turn out, the last leaving the barracks five minutes later; of these:

Gun no.	Time reported ready	Site
1	7.00 p.m.	Aldwych WC2
2	8.20 p.m. – problems 7.35 p.m.	Higham Hill E17
3	7.45 p.m.	Manor Park E12
4	7.24 p.m.	Becton E16
5	7.24 p.m.	Streatham SW16
6	7.20 p.m.	Clapham SW4

Operational requirements meant that some of these sites were replacements for earlier ones while others in turn gave way to new ones. The move in general was to shift the mobile gun positions from north of London southwards and a representative list of re-sited locations must include:

Finchley, which was replaced by Wandsworth
Palmer's Green, transferring to Clapham
Wandsworth Flats to Beckenham (Kent)
Becton to Grove Park

Clearly, it was assumed that the answer to the problem of protecting London by means of mobile anti-aircraft guns was regarded as having been solved by the middle of 1917, when fourteen guns were reported to be in use, comprising:

4 French 75mm quick-firing 'auto-canon' on French-designed mountings
1 British 3in, 20-cwt high-velocity q/f high-angle gun on a Daimler with a mobile mounting (type unspecified)
1 British 3in, 20-cwt high-velocity q/f high-angle gun on a trailer
8 3-pdr high-velocity q/f high-angle guns on Lancia mobile mountings
4 Searchlights on Tilling-Stevens chassis. These were of 60cm diameter, with dynamos capable of powering the light while the vehicle was stationary.
Guns could also be alternatively mounted on Peerless or Thornycroft 3-ton lorries and searchlights on Dennis 3-tonners which had been built by Stevens.

That the Royal Navy had been responsible for the defence of the homeland against aerial attack was somewhat fancifully explained. The illustrious service was merely fulfilling its traditional role, but the reason was rather more prosaic, being more due to the fact that the Army was at full stretch overseas at the time enemy attacks were begun. In 1917 the situation had altered and the Army assumed responsibility, Major General Edward Ashmore in overall command of air defences from 5 August. He recognised the outstanding work that had been performed by Rawlinson, now a Commander, RN, and retained him. He nevertheless had to change his service, becoming a Lieutenant-Colonel in the Royal Garrison Artillery.

Indeed there was deemed to be little need for radical change and during 1917–18 the West Sub-Command of London's Anti-Aircraft Defences constituted twenty fixed gun positions, all in immediate communication by telephone with Headquarters at Putney. The gun-sites were each manned by about twenty soldiers and were as follows:

Acton	Horsend Hill
Beckenham	Hounslow
Bromley	Kenton
Croydon	Morden
Dulwich	Norbiton
Enfield	Richmond
Grove Park	Staines
Hampton	Wandsworth
Hanwell	Watford
Hayes (Mx)	Windsor

Each of these in general had, in turn, a pair of searchlights, the first termed a 'fighting light' and the second, more distant, an 'advanced light'. Additionally, each gun was usually accompanied by a pair of observers, again, one near and one distant from the gun, their duty being to observe the shell bursts and therefore the accuracy of the shooting. These were men were usually situated at a location offering a wide field of view, either from its height or lack of obstruction. There were forty-eight of these.

The searchlights were to prove something of a problem, not from the standard of illumination that they gave but from the fact that from the total of thirty-six, they were of varying sizes and of five different makes, each with its differing system of starting the dynamo, ability to run continuously and care procedure.

However, among these there existed a type that was especially interesting, an example of one being the Purley (Surrey) Light which was for the sake of mobility mounted on the upper deck of a open-top tram which would turn out from the depot each night when a warning was received and make its way to the end of the line at a cross-roads, about half a mile away. The vehicle was painted entirely grey, had its windows boarded over and when not in use, its light was protected by a canvas cover. Communication with Headquarters was by means of standard Army Telephone sets which could be plugged into 'jacks' (plug points) one being fastened to each alternate standard carrying the overhead wires along the route. Six such trams are known to have operated in the Metropolitan Police area.

The differences in chosen gun sites are typified by these, consecutively Pickhurst Mead – the grounds of a nineteenth-century mansion; Gonville Road – the undeveloped end of a housing estate, and the Long Walk in Windsor Great Park, two others being allocated to Ilford.

The London detachment from the Mobile Brigade was, however, not the only one, as was clear to anyone who saw (a little after dawn on what was to prove one of the beautiful mornings that marked the last days of August 1916) a convoy consisting of twelve mobile guns, three mobile searchlights and twenty other vehicles such as ammunition wagons and motor-cycles making for the Great North Road out of the metropolis, their duty being to provide mobile anti-aircraft protection to a section of the East Coast.

Arriving at North Walsham an hour after midday, a temporary camp was set up, a permanent headquarters being established at Bacton the next day and while a force consisting of a pair of 75mm guns just north of this point, a 3-pounder was stationed south of Mundesley with a searchlight to the north and another gun of the same type at Watch House with a further searchlight at Walcot gap. The remainder of the new Mobile Brigade being spaced at 1 mile intervals to guard Sandringham House, the residence of Edward VII's widow Alexandra, the Queen Mother, the guns being supported by the remaining searchlight, ahead of them.

At 8.45 p.m. on 2 September, a warning of the sighting of the leader of an approaching force of fifteen airships was received and the first of the guns and searchlights left headquarters for their designated positions, all being reported ready for action by 9.20 p.m., and although 170 bombs were officially logged as having been dropped that night, twenty-three of them falling in the sea, and a heavy barrage was put up, the intended target of the night was London. One of the raiders passed into history as the first airship destroyed over British soil – Schutte-Lanz SL11 which fell to the fire of Lieutenant William Leefe Robinson over Cuffley.

In addition to these facts on the unique Mobile Brigades, we have some recollections of life with one of the fixed gun positions, Mr F.L. Mayhew being posted to the gun at Cuffley, which fell under the North Sub-Command, in February/March 1916, where he chiefly recalls the 60-cms searchlight 'advanced light', powered by a Kelvin marine generator mounted on a lorry of which he says:

The exhibition of former-enemy arms and aeroplanes continued into the years of peace, this Friedrichshafen GIIIa (1429/16) in St James' Park, London, being an example. It had first been shown as part of the Imperial War Museum's exhibition of enemy aircraft in the Crystal Palace.

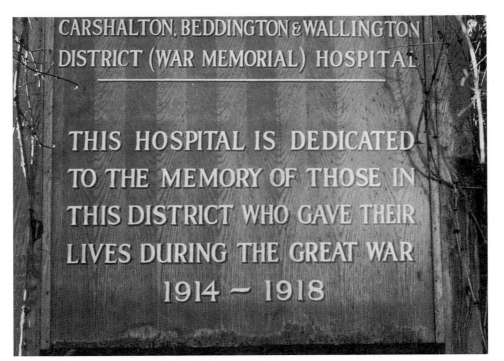

Some areas remembered those who had died in the 'war to end wars' with stone memorials, others conceived memorials of a more practical nature, as witness this hospital in Surrey. (Author)

there was very little room left to get between the flywheel and the side to enable the trip starter to be operated. Backfires were not uncommon so the handle was dropped pretty smartly... The searchlight was mounted on the ground and a platform of four planks enabled the operator to manipulate the lamp, but when the beam was vertical, he had to step gingerly round – or rather across – the corner to bring it down on the other side, as reverse gear had not been thought of.' Communication between the engine [dynamo] and it, was by ordinary Field Telephone or even loud shouting!.. One occasion we picked up a Zeppelin in our beam flying over London.

Equally frustrating was the time when, having just warmed up the engine of a lorry, the prevailing blizzard blew down an elm tree on to it during the occasion when the weather:

...did enormous damage along the Great North Road and elsewhere. One the following morning I had to walk in to report to HQ that we were out of action [and] we more or less dug our way to the billet for breakfast on many days... [through the snow] We were actually positioned on Law's Farm... Our gun – manned by Hants and Dorset gunners – fired about four rounds [when a Zeppelin was sighted] and then had to pack up if the angle was above 60° which would have knocked out the bottom boards of the lorry on which it was mounted.

Thus was created the structure of Britain's gun defences as the end of the First World War approached. The Royal Naval Volunteer Reserve Anti-Aircraft Corps, which had in effect laid its foundations, was destined to continue its existence until the beginning of 1919, although by now it had long become a full-time service and been extended to other cities, before widening its operational scope to the manning of such vessels as the anti-aircraft kite-balloon ship HMS *Manica* which saw service as a gunnery spotter as far away as the coast of German East Africa in 1916–17. Some twenty years later civilians realised that the end of all this was no more than the half-time whistle in some ghastly killing match, but how their tribulations and sufferings were to be resumed is, sadly, another story.

AFTERWORD

CIVILIAN SOLDIERS

There is no doubt that there existed in England a very real fear of invasion. This was so great that not long after the outbreak of hostilities in August 1914 the bombardment of Scarborough, Whitby and Hartlepool on 16 December heralded something of this nature, with the result that 300,000 troops had already been deployed to defend the North East coast during the previous month, a time when tides and wind seemed most to favour such an attack.

Aware of the potential situation, the public had already taken the first steps to meet such a threat when Member of the House of Commons Percy Harris (Liberal) rose to propose the formation of a volunteer force to defend the capital, if a successful enemy landing was made, a suggestion which received two days later the support of such notables as Sir Arthur Conan Doyle and H.G. Wells. In fact this proposal was swiftly welcomed by many people and just as quickly rejected by others, among whom was Lord Kitchener who was psychologically devoted to preserving a 'macho' public image.

Nevertheless, Town Guards and Volunteer Defences were already in the course of formation in at least five counties so that, faced with a *fait accompli*, Kitchener had no alternative but to accept the matter and order the establishment of a civilian training corps in mid-November.

The result was swift, allegedly the first such body appearing in Wandsworth before the end of the month having been founded at a Council Meeting on 19 November, its strength within a few days numbering 305 members who were seemingly drilled in civilian clothes with dummy firearms, adopting the title of 'Home Defence Volunteers'. A similar force was known as the 'Volunteer Training Corps', while the range of names by which the new organisation was known was unofficially extended with the passage of time becoming known as the Infantry Training Corps, Volunteer Training Corps, Volunteer Force, or just Volunteers.

Officers and men of No.4 regiment (IOW) Voluntary Training Corps. (Courtesy T.C. Hudson collection)

The earliest known photograph of Walthamstow VTC at rifle practice before the wearing of regulation uniform. (Author's collection)

In time uniforms were issued, these being a shade of grey not unlike that worn by the enemy, together with stiff-peaked cap unlike the softer type worn by regular troops. Boots were black and on the right sleeve was worn a wide, red brassard bearing the letters in black 'GR' which was humorously interpreted by some as standing for 'Grandpa's Regiment' or 'Genuine Relics'. Later this brassard was replaced by a khaki one marked only with a red crown.

Eventually there was to take place perhaps the greatest change in the structure of these units when they were affiliated to local units of the regular Army, but this was not to last long, since with the war over the Corps was officially dispersed toward the end of 1920 – although a number of units were to survive as rifle clubs, this preserving the very high standards of shooting many members had attained during the war. One writer has related a memory of the work of Dorset's 4th Volunteer Regiment during those years, saying, 'It consisted of men too old, too young or too unfit for other military service [a description not borne out by photographs], commanded by Colonel Frank Hankinson, a local estate agent', before abandoning cynicism and outlining the units' work.

Chief among these responsibilities was the patrolling of the cliffs and sea-front between sunset and dawn and keeping the beach clear together with ensuring that the dim-out regulations were kept. Patrols for this work were carried out by pairs of men unarmed except by the carriage of swordsticks during the hours of duty which were divided into two watches, the first from dusk to 2 a.m., the second between 2 a.m. and dawn when they would snatch a few hours sleep wrapped in a blanket on the wooden floor, the late turn having satisfied their hunger with thick slices of bread with cheese.

In public, firearms were never carried, although off-duty honing their shooting skills with live ammunition was keenly contested, using Lee-Enfield rifles, the rifle clubs which many became after the Armistice maintaining these standards for many years.

John Cyril Hudson, private of the VTC, wearing the grey uniform with red arm band, c.1916. (Courtesy T.C. Hudson collection)

APPENDICES

Appendix One

Procurement and Distribution of Searchlight-Trams

In 1916, two double-deck trams were commandeered by the War Office to be converted and trialled in towns as mobile searchlight carriers.

This called for fairly considerable alteration, the main requirement being the housing of a 60cm searchlight on the open top deck. The closed lower deck was to be used to accommodate a quantity of heavy equipment, and also to provide shelter for the crew, although a part of the upper deck was also used for this, in a covered portion added at one end.

The type of car chosen was that known as Type X, reportedly those individually numbered 25 and 34, this pair believed to be those described as being requisitioned at about this time from LUT (London United Tramways), which is known to have had a surplus.

Total cars requisitioned and sources:

CCT	(Croydon Corporation Tramways)	2. Only one used, the other reserved as a spare.
IDC	(Ilford Urban District Tramways)	2
LUT	(London United Tramways)	2
MET	(Metropolitan Electric Tramways)	6
	Known total used	11

Ordinary crewmen were, in fact, soldiers drawn from the Royal Engineers, while motormen had formerly served with the South Shields and London and Tyne Electrical Company of the Royal Engineers.

Trams were converted and introduced as a matter of urgency to form a ring of mobile searchlights some 10 to 12 miles out from the capital, as a result of increased enemy activity at night.

Model of a tram carrying a searchlight on its upper deck. (Courtesy David Voice)

Appendix Two

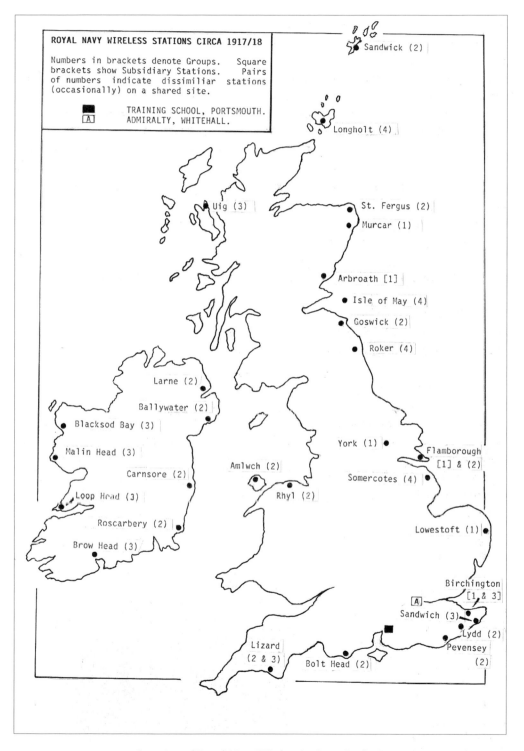

ROYAL NAVY WIRELESS STATIONS CIRCA 1917/18

Numbers in brackets denote Groups.   Square
brackets show Subsidiary Stations.   Pairs
of numbers indicate dissimiliar stations
(occasionally) on a shared site.

■ TRAINING SCHOOL, PORTSMOUTH.
Ⓐ ADMIRALTY, WHITEHALL.

Sandwick (2)

Longholt (4)

Uig (3)

St. Fergus (2)

Murcar (1)

Arbroath [1]

Isle of May (4)

Goswick (2)

Roker (4)

Larne (2)

Ballywater (2)

Blacksod Bay (3)

Malin Head (3)

Carnsore (2)

Amlwch (2)

York (1)

Flamborough [1] & (2)

Somercotes (4)

Loop Head (3)

Rhyl (2)

Roscarbery (2)

Brow Head (3)

Lowestoft (1)

Birchington [1] & 3]

Ⓐ

Sandwich (3)

Lydd (2)

Pevensey (2)

Lizard (2 & 3)

Bolt Head (2)

Location of Royal Navy Wireless Stations. (Author)

Last Post

The Cenotaph (literally an 'empty tomb') had been conceived as a temporary centre for the nation's homage, and was erected in connection with the Peace Procession of 1919. This was to the design of Sir Edwin Lutyens and was constructed from wood and plaster.

Later, the decision was made to build an identical, permanent, stone structure. This was achieved, and the new memorial was first used in 1920.

This photograph shows the memorial after the closure of the ceremonials three years later. Earlier suggestions that it be re-erected in the Mall had been rejected.

Opposite: The work of Sir Edwin Landseer Lutyens R.A., the Cenotaph was first raised in Whitehall as a focal point for the Peace Celebrations of July 1919 when it was a simple structure of wood and plaster, but in 1920 it was replaced by the present identical stone monument. It is seen here following Armistice Day, 1923. (Author's collection)

INDEX

If you are interested in purchasing other books published by Tempus, or in case you have difficulty finding any Tempus books in your local bookshop, you can also place orders directly through our website www.tempus-publishing.com